THE
COMPLETE PLAYS OF
THE WAKEFIELD MASTER

in a new version for
reading and performance
by
John Russell Brown

HEINEMANN
LONDON

Heinemann Educational Books Ltd
22 Bedford Square, London WC1B 3HH

LONDON EDINBURGH MELBOURNE AUCKLAND
HONG KONG SINGAPORE KUALA LUMPUR NEW DELHI
NAIROBI JOHANNESBURG IBADAN KINGSTON
EXETER (NH) PORT OF SPAIN

British Library Cataloguing in Publication Data

Brown, John Russell
 The complete plays of The Wakefield Master.
 I. Title   II. Wakefield Master
 822'.914   PR6052.R/

 ISBN 0-435-23138-3

Typeset by The Castlefield Press of Northampton
and printed in Great Britain by
Biddles Ltd, of Kings Lynn and Guildford

Contents

Introduction

No pageants from the medieval English Mystery Cycles, which tell the story of the world from its beginnings to the Last Judgement, are more valued today than six, probably written by one man, which are preserved in a manuscript written in the second half of the fifteenth century and now safely lodged in the Huntington Library, California. Allusions and placenames, together with 'Wakefield' in the titles of the two pageants, connect the manuscript with the Yorkshire town which is known to have had performances of mystery plays from 1554 to 1576: they took place on Corpus Christi day, the Thursday following Trinity Sunday (which was eight weeks after Easter Day). The manuscript shows that this cycle had thirty-two pageants, but the six outstanding ones have become known separately as the plays of 'The Wakefield Master'. All six are written with similar linguistic vitality and dramatic skill, and verbal echoes between them are signs of common authorship. These plays tell the stories of Cain and Abel, Noah and the Flood, Herod and the Massacre of the Innocents, the Buffetting of Christ before the High Priests and the Nativity of Christ, in two different versions. The *Cain* is probably a re-working of an earlier version, for it is mostly in irregular metre rather than the nine-line stanza that distinguishes the other plays. The *Second Shepherds' Play* is the most famous of them all and there must be very few anthologies of early English drama that do not include it.

All six plays of the Master, and some stanzas that he may have contributed to other pageants, can be read in the original, fifteenth-century form in scholarly editions of the complete cycle, known either as the Wakefield Plays or the Towneley Plays (after the Lancashire family who owned the manuscript from the early seventeenth-century until recent times). There was an edition by the Surtees Society in 1836, edited by J. Gordon and J. Hunter, and another by the Early English Text Society in 1897, edited by George England and A. W. Pollard. In 1958, the six plays of the Wakefield Master were edited separately by A. C. Cawley for Manchester University Press, a publication to which all subsequent editors and scholars must owe a great debt.

One and, occasionally, more of the Master's plays have been printed in anthologies, both in their original form and in modernized, and often abridged, versions. And a modernization of the whole cycle by Martial Rose has also been published in 1962. But what has been missing until now is an edition of the six plays by the Wakefield Master in a version that is faithful to the original but provides a text that can be read today without difficulty and can be used in performances for modern audiences. That is what the present edition provides.

This Version and the Original
When the National Theatre in London set about staging a play drawn from the English mystery cycles it commissioned a poet, Tony Harrison, to write *The Passion* based on pageants from the York Cycle. But when the director, Bill Bryden, extended the production by the addition of another play starting with the Creation and continuing until the Birth of Christ and the Massacre of the Innocents, he adapted sections from the Chester Cycle as well as the York and used the plays of the Wakefield Master for Cain and Abel, Noah and the Ark and the Shepherds. This time the production was based directly on the medieval texts, without rewriting by a contemporary poet. So *The Passion*, Part One (Creation to Nativity) opened at the Edinburgh Festival in 1980 and, as *The Nativity*, moved to the Cottesloe Theatre, London later that year. It subsequently visited Cologne and Rome.

The new version of the works of the Wakefield Master which is published here stems from the National Theatre production and sections of it have already been incorporated in *The Passion* Part One, the text of that N.T. play which is published by Rex Collings (London 1980).

The brief was to prepare a script for rehearsals. Words that have lost all meaning had to be changed, and numerous puns and allusions could not be retained. But every effort was made to preserve the tones, rhythms, rhymes, alliteration and 'feel' of the original. Some words that are now archaic, regional or even obsolete were found to gain new life in the context of the rehearsals and were therefore retained in the modern version. (In this published text a glossary gives help with any word that is not current today.) Dialect variations were almost wholly abandoned, but colloquial phrasing and much of the original syntax were preserved so that the text could be spoken in a variety of regional accents while retaining a north-eastern basis. The double test that was applied everywhere to this version was whether it kept as much of the original as possible while providing a text that actors would enjoy using for a modern audience.

Staging the Plays

Each play can last between thirty and fifty minutes, depending on how elaborate, inventive and musical the performance; with judicious cutting much less time is needed. The smallest possible cast for each play varies from four to ten, but in all cases more actors can be used for supporting roles, and members of the audience can be encouraged to participate.

There is some evidence that Corpus Christi plays were performed at Wakefield on pageant waggons taken round the town in procession to a number of different locations. But nothing in the texts of the Master's plays demands the use of such a waggon. They can be performed in any arena, surrounded on all or some sides by an audience. Small scenic units or stage-properties can represent the more specific locations that are necessary, such as the hill on which Noah's Wife sits to spin, the stable at Bethlehem, Herod's throne-room or the High Priest's law-court. The Ark itself has to be assembled in view of the audience and that can best be done on an open stage. Perhaps the most elaborate feature needed for the staging of the plays is some provision for God and the Angel to appear at a higher level, and for Cain to make his public pronouncement. Notes on the basic requirements for this kind of staging are prefixed to the text of each play in this edition.

At the Assembly Hall, Edinburgh, and in the Cottesloe Theatre, short versions of three of the plays were performed in a central area around which the audience stood or sat as they wished. This very simple 'promenade' staging proved eminently practical. It encouraged the interaction between players and audience that the text requires and it heightened the variety of the drama in *The Passion,* Part One: the formality of some ritualistic scenes, the ordered violence of Herod's soldiers, the simple realism and reverence of the shepherds' worship of the Christ-child, all brought about a new configuration of the audience and a new kind of involvement.

Within one continuous speech a single intention or reaction may be repeated in several different statements, each one varied a little as if viewed from a changing perspective. One way of presenting such a speech is to cut some of the repetitions, but if the plays are staged in an arena or on a centrally placed waggon, the actor can address each repetition to a different section of the audience and so maintain, and develop, interest all the way through.

The acting needs to be bold, simple, honest and self-sufficient. Characters make strong entries and are explicit about their thoughts and feelings. The dialogue is by turns colloquial, racy, and studied, but it is usually short-phrased and sharply pointed: given time to breathe and make each varied impact, it responds well to fully individualized but simple performance. The plays start with direct address to the audience in which the main characters establish themselves with the audience as well as with the situation of the drama. During the course of the plays, characters speak to the audience telling jokes, giving advice or information, asking for reactions, admonishing attention or silence. They remain 'in character', but the National Theatre production showed that the actors have to be ready for all kinds of response and sometimes for impromptu repartee.

The long-lined stanzas, with numerous rhymes and alliteration, together with the preponderance of monosyllables, necessitate a clear, measured but energetic delivery which suits well with this kind of performance. The very short fifth lines, always followed by three lines with two or three stresses only and a single rhyme, and then a concluding line with a rhyme that ties it back to the fifth, prevent any heaviness or too great regularity; so there is a spring to even the longer speeches, and many metrical surprises. When a stanza is split between several speakers a great variety of pitch and tone can be used without loss of rhythm or forward drive.

Opportunity occurs for processions and journeys from one location to another in which actors can improvise and develop their basic physical performances. Other activity includes eating, drinking, ploughing, driving imaginary sheep, spinning, rocking a baby asleep, legal consultations in impressive tomes, saying prayers, singing and fighting: all of this is integral to the drama and repays lively and true performance. The massacre of the innocents and the 'buffetting' of Christ call for violent action, but the author has cunningly opposed the silence of Christ and the helplessness of the infants to the cruel humour and relish of their oppressors, and so these scenes can be staged with a measure of formality or slow-motion ritual without loss of energy or dramatic immediacy. They communicate more than the horror.

There are plenty of occasions when music can be introduced into a performance, not only when the characters sing. The entry of Herod can be to trumpets and his Knights move off to military music: God may well be given his own music to establish a new perspective and different reality. A drum or wood-wind instrument can accompany the various journeys and other appropriate music can represent the passage of time, when the Shepherds fall asleep, the Counsellors consult their books or the level of the flood waters changes.

The building of the Ark or the driving of Cain's ploughing team can be supported and shaped by strongly rhythmical music, while one way of staging the massacre or the buffetting is to control the violent action by slow-paced deliberate music. Mystery plays derived from church services and so the original performances may have relied greatly on this element of theatre.

The Plays

Very few students can read these plays in their original text without taking time to seek out the meanings of difficult words and distinguish grammatical forms and dialect variations. Such study leads to a greater appreciation of the verbal finesse of the Wakefield Master, but it can obscure other qualities of his work — not least their astonishing dramatic vitality. To make this accessible to a far wider public is one of the purposes of this present edition. Here the text can be read aloud, with little or no preparation, and so the dialogue may start into its proper life. This text is also ready for performance and so long as the acting is clear and vital — qualities that are not the possession of professional actors only — they may be staged with a minimum of technical equipment or support. Even a silent reading, because it can be fluent and responsive, will give a lively impression in the imagination.

Readers who are accustomed only to modern plays should be prepared for a greater variation of tone than usual. Serious and comic are close together; indeed they seem to touch, as a joke reveals its earnest or a solemn moment its incongruity. Even the Angel's song, a blazing light from Heaven or the world's first murder have their comic aspects, while Noah's clumsy prayer and Herod's rodomontade and bluster touch upon deepest issues.

Readers should allow themselves time to visualize the action required by the text; without doing this they will skip over silent moments that have narrative and thematic importance, or fail to recognize how the dialogue has changed in tempo and rhythm. The clearest example of this is the silence of Christ when he is being interrogated and tormented, but in a lesser degree reactions to cold and hunger, the sustaining silence after Abel's death, the search for a sheep in Mak's cottage, the spreading out of an imaginary feast or the slow waking from sleep and the urgent rocking of a cradle all illuminate variations in the dialogue.

Of course, a knowledge of the biblical source of the plays adds further understanding, especially in the light of medieval exigesis which saw episodes of Old Testament as prophesying or prefiguring the events of the New, or repeating earlier events. So Cain re-enacts the Fall of Lucifer and prefigures the Last Judgement; Abel is a 'type' of Christ and his sacrificial lamb an emblem of the crucifixion. In a sense the whole biblical narrative is implicit in each play so that anachronistic references to Christ's birth or death are not out of place in episodes from the Old Testament story, and quotations from the prophets are natural in the mouth of unlettered shepherds.

The Wakefield Master introduced other echoes or 'types' of his own invention in the incidents which he elaborated from the biblical outline: the quarrel of Noah and his wife repeats the differences between Adam and Eve; the sheep in Mak's cradle is a type of Christ (especially when he and his wife say they will eat it); the shared meal of bread and wine in the *First Shepherds' Play* is a type of Christ feeding the thousands in the wilderness and of the Eucharist.

Non-biblical sources can also be recognized in the plays: proverbs, ancient jokes and games, folk-tales and reactions to topical social issues, such as bad weather, bad masters and locally-brewed ale. Most important of all, perhaps, is their author's strong sense of individual character that brings to dramatic life farm-labourers and lawyers, a young mother and a shrewish wife, servants and lords. Even God and the Angel have been given speeches that are imagined thoroughly from the speaker's standpoint. A reader should be ready to recognize an everyday and personal reality in these plays, as well as ancient narrative, doctrine, exegesis and rituals, and a masterly use of language and theatre.

Characters
PICKHARNESS, Cain's Boy
CAIN
ABEL
GOD

Cain's ploughing team, of four horses and four oxen, may be represented by eight actors or by more or less simple models of large or small size.

Staging
An open area, surrounded by the audience is used for the fields. To one side is a raised place for offering sacrifice; stooks of corn are nearby. A device is needed to emit bright light from the altar fire and, later, black smoke.

A higher level is required for God's entry. This could also be the rostrum from which Cain makes his proclamation; alternatively a further raised stage could be provided, opposite to the place of sacrifice.

I The Killing of Abel

Enter PICKHARNESS, *blowing a horn.*

PICKHARNESS:
    All hail, all hail, both blithe and glad,
    For here come I, a merry lad!
    Now shut your din, my master bad,
        Or else the devil you speed!
    Wat ye not I come before?
    Whoever jangles any more
    Must blow my hole, my black bore,
    Both behind and before,
        Till his teeth bleed.
    Fellows, here I you forbid   10
        To make neither noise nor cry:
    Whoso is so hardy to do that deed,
        The devil hang him up to dry!

    Godlings, I am a full great man;
    My master is a bold yeoman:
        Full well ye all him ken.
    If he starts with you to strive,
    Be sure that you will never thrive;
    And I trow, by God alive,
        Some of you are his men.   20
    But shut your lips over your teen,
        Varlets everyone!
    And if my master come, welcome him then.
        Farewell, for I am gone. *Exit.*

Enter CAIN, *ploughing.*

CAIN:
    Gee up Greenhorn! Ware out, Dun.
    Draw on! God give you ill fortune!

Ye stand as though ye were fallen in swoon:
    Will ye no further, mare?
Ware! Let's see how Dun will draw:
Up bitch! Up! Pull on a thraw!   30
What! It seems of me none stand in awe!
    I say, Dunning, go fare!
Aha! God give thee sorrow and care!   ·
Lo! Now heard she what I said.
    But yet art thou the worst mare
To plough, that ever I bred.

Ho, Pickharness, ho! Come here! Look alive!

Enter PICKHARNESS.

PICKHARNESS:
    I forfend, God wot, that ever thou thrive!

CAIN:
    What boy, shall I both hold and drive?
    Hearest thou not how I cry?   40

PICKHARNESS (*To the ploughing-team*):
    Say, Moll and Stott, will ye not go?
    Leming, Morell, Whitehorn, ho!
    Now will ye not see how they hie?

CAIN:
    God give thee sorrow, boy. Lack of feed is the cause.

PICKHARNESS (*Sarcastically*):
    Their provender, sir, you see, I place at their arse,
    And tie them fast by their necks,
    Putting many stones in their racks.

CAIN:
    Thou shalt buy that on thy cheeks! *Strikes him.*

PICKHARNESS:
    And have that again right! *Strikes back.*

CAIN:
    I am thy master. Wilt thou fight?   50

PICKHARNESS:
    Yea, with the same measure and weight:
    What I borrow will I requite.

CAIN:

>Have done! and call out with thy might
>>So we can plough this land.

PICKHARNESS:

>Gee up, Morell! Draw on, hite!
>(*Aside*) And let the plough stand. *He takes the team off.*

Enter ABEL.

ABEL:

>God, as he both may and can,
>Speed thee, brother, and thy man.

CAIN:

>Come kiss my arse! I will not ban:
>>But away from here is your welcome.   60
>Thou should ha' stayed till thou were called.
>Come near and either drive or hold,
>>And kiss the devil's bum.
>Go graze thy sheep, under and out,
>>For that to thee is lief.

ABEL:

>Brother, there is none about
>>To wish thee any grief.

>But, brother dear, hear my saw:
>It is the custom of our law,
>That all the workers that are wise   70
>Shall worship God with sacrifice.
>Our father us bad and gave us command,
>A tithe of our goods should be burnt with brand.
>Come forth, brother, and let us gang
>To worship God: we stay too long.
>>Give we to Him part of our fee,
>>Corn or cattle, whatever it be.

>And therefore, brother, let us wend,
>And first cleanse us from the fiend
>>Ere we make the sacrifice;   80
>Then bliss withouten any end
>>Get we for our true service,

>From Him that is our soul's good leach.

CAIN:

> Ho! Let forth your geese: the fox to them will preach.
> How long wilt thou me appeach
>> With thy sermoning?
> Hold thy tongue, yet I say,
> Down there at the place where women play!
> Or have done, in the devil's way,
>> With thy vain carping.   90
>
> Should I leave my plough and everything
> And go with thee to make off'ring?
> Nay, thou findst me not so mad.
> Go to the devil, and say I bad!
> What gives God to thee, to praise him so?
> He gives me nought but sorrow and woe.

ABEL:

> Cain, leave this vain carping,
> For God gives thee all thy living.

CAIN:

> Yet borrowed I never a farthing
> Of Him! — here is my hand!   100

ABEL:

> Brother, as our elders gave command,
> A tithe should we offer with our hand,
> A tenth of our goods to be burnt with the brand.

CAIN:

> My farthing is still in priest's hand,
>> From last time I offered.

ABEL:

> Dear brother, let us not here stand:
>> I wish our tithe were proffered.

CAIN:

> Wei! From what should I tithe, dear brother?
> For I am each year worse than other —
> This is truth; it is no other.   110
> My winnings are only mean:
> No wonder if I be so lean.
> Full long to Him I may complain,

For, by Him that me dearly bought,
I trow that He will lend me nought.

ABEL:

> Yes, all the good that thou has won
> Of God's grace is but a loan.

CAIN:

Loans He to me? May profit come to thee so!
For He has ever yet been my foe.
For, had He my friend been, 120
Otherways it had been seen.
When all men's corn was fair in field,
Then was mine not worth a needle.
When I should sow, and lacked the seed,
And of corn had full great need,
Then gave He me none of His;
No more will I give Him of this.
> You may hold me to blame
> Unless I serve Him just the same.

ABEL:

Dear brother, say not so, 130
But let us forth together go.
Good brother, let us soon wend;
By staying here we will not mend.

CAIN:

Yea, yea! Thy words are waste!
The devil me speed if I have haste,
As long as I may live,
To deal out part or give,
Either to God or yet to man,
Of any good that ever I won.
For had I given away my good, 140
Then might I go with tattered hood;
And it is better hold what I have
Than beg from door to door, and crave.

ABEL:

Brother, come forth, in God's name:
I am full 'feared that we get blame.
Hie we fast till we be there.

CAIN:

> Wei! Run on, in the devil's name, before!
> For God's sake, I hold thee mad!
> Think'st thou now that I list gad
> To give away my all or aught?   150
> The devil him speed that me so taught!
> What need had I my labour to lose,
> To wear out my shoes and tear my hose?

ABEL:

> Dear brother, it were great wonder
> That I and thou should go asunder:
> It would our father amaze greatly.
> Are we not brothers, thou and I?

CAIN:

> Cry on, cry on if you think it good!
> Here's my troth: I hold thee wode.
> Whether he be blithe or wroth,   160
> To share my good I am full loth.
> I have gone oft in softer wise
> Whene'er I thought profit would rise.
> But well I see to go there's need:
> So wend on before — ill may thou speed! —
> Since anyhow we have to go.

ABEL:

> Dear brother, why says thou so?
> But go we forth both together;
> Blessed be God, we have fair weather.

They go to the place of sacrifice; ABEL *takes a sheep with him.*

CAIN:

> Lay down thy bundle upon this hill.   170

ABEL:

> Forsooth, brother, so I will.
> And God of heaven, take it for good.

CAIN:

> Now offer first thy livelihood.

ABEL:

> God that shaped both earth and sky
> I pray to Thee, Thou hear my cry:

Now take with thanks, if Thy will be,
The tithe that I offer here to Thee;
For I give it with good intent
To Thee, my Lord, that all has sent.
I burn it now with steadfast thought,   180
In worship of Him that all has wrought.

The altar fire blazes with a bright light.

CAIN:
Rise! Let me now, since thou has done.
Lord of heaven, hear Thou my boon.
And God forbid You offer to me
Either your thanks or courtesy;
For, as I may use these two shanks,
It is full sore without my thanks
The tithe that here I give to Thee
Of corn that newly grows for me.
But now begin I in my turn,   190
Since I must need my tenth to burn.

He starts to count the first ten sheaves, keeping the best for himself.

One sheaf, *one*; and this makes two:
Yet neither can I spare for You.
Two, two; now this is three;
Yea, this also shall stay with me,
For I will chose the best to have —
This is my due — of all, this sheaf.
Come on, come on! Four, lo, here!
Better grew I none this year.
At proper time I sowed fair corn,   200
Yet was it such when it was shorn:
Thistles and briers — yea, great plenty! —
And all kind of weeds that might be.
Four sheaves, four: lo, this makes five —
If I deal out thus, I'll never thrive!
Five, and six; now this is seven —
But this goes never to the God of heaven.
Nor none of these four, by my might,
Shall ever come in to God's sight.
Seven, seven; now this is eight.   210

ABEL:

> Cain, brother, thou call on God's hate.

CAIN:

> Wei! Therefore is it that I say
> I will not deal my good away.
> If I this tenth to God did lend
> Then would thou say He were my friend;
> But I think not, by my hood,
> To part so lightly with my good.
> Wei! Eight, eight, and nine; and ten is this:
> Wei! This may we best miss. *He chooses the smallest sheaf.*
> Shall I give that that lies there?   220
> It goes against mine heart full sore.

ABEL:

> Cain! Give a tenth from all between. . . .

CAIN:

> Ah well! Twelve, fifteen, and sixteen. . . .
>
> *He counts the next ten sheaves very quickly.*

ABEL:

> Cain, thou tithe wrong, and take the worst.

CAIN:

> Wei! Come near, and hide mine eyen.
> In the dark hour be quiet at last!
> Or else do thou wish I should wink?
> Then shall I do no wrong, methink.
>
> *He shuts his eyes until he has finished counting.*
>
> Let me see now how it is.
>   Lo, yet I am well paid!   230
> I tithéd wondrous well by guess,
>   So fairly have I laid.

ABEL:

> Cain, of God methink thou has no dread.

CAIN:

> He will get no more, if the devil speed;
> Not as much as a hand may reap.
> That one there He got full cheap:

Not as mickle, great or small,
As He might wipe His arse withall.
For that, and this that lies here,
Have cost me very dear.   240
Ere it was shorn and brought to stack,
It gave me many a weary back.
Therefore ask me no more of this,
For I have given what my will is.

ABEL:

Cain, I tell thee tithe aright,
For dread of Him that sits on height.

CAIN:

How that I tithe, reckon never a deal,
But tend thy scabby sheep still;
For if thou fault with my tithe take,
It will be the worse for thy sake.   250
Thou would I gave Him this sheaf? or this sheaf?
No, neither of these two for Him will I leave.
But take this. Now has He two, *He takes a second sheaf.*
And for my soul now must it go.
But it goes sore against my will,
Even if He should like full ill.

ABEL:

Cain, thou should the tithe tend
So that God of heaven be thy friend.

CAIN:

My friend? No; not unless He will!
I have never done but good skill.   260
If He be never so my foe,
I am advised give Him no more.
But change thy conscience, as I do mine.
Do thou not tithe thy measly swine?

ABEL:

If thou tithe right, thou good will find.

CAIN:

Yea, and kiss the devil's arse behind!
The devil hang thee by the neck!
How that I tithe, never thou reck.
Will thou not yet hold thy peace?

Of this jangling, I counsel cease.   270
And tithe I well or tithe I ill,
Bear thee even and speak with skill.
But now, since thou has tithed thine,
Now will I set fire to mine. CAIN'*s offering will not burn.*
Wei! Out, alas! Help to blow!
It will not burn for me, I trow.
Puff! This smoke does me much shame —
Now, burn, in the devil's name!

Black smoke appears.

Ah! What devil of hell is it?
My lungs almost had been split.   280
Had I blown but one blast more
I had been choked right sore.
It stank like the devil in hell,
So longer there might I not dwell.

ABEL:

Cain, this is not worth one leek;
Thy tithe should burn without this stink.

CAIN:

Come kiss the devil right in the arse!
Because of *thee*, it burns the worse.
I would that it were in thy throat,
Fire and sheaf, and every sprout.   290

GOD *appears above.*

GOD:

Cain, why art thou such a rebel
Against thy brother, Abel?
To flite and chide there is no need.
If thou tithe right, thou getst thy meed;
And be thou sure, if thou tithe false,
Thou shall be paid with nothing else. *He withdraws.*

CAIN:

Why, who is that hob-over-the-wall?
Wei! Who was that piped so small?
Come go we hence from perils all:
      God is out of his wit.   300

>Come forth, Abel, and let us wend;
>Methink God is not my friend.
>>Away, then, must I flit.

CAIN:

>Ah, Cain, brother, that is ill done.

CAIN:

>No, but go we hence soon.
>And if I may, I shall be
>Where e'er God shall *not* me see.

ABEL:

>Dear brother, I will fare
>To field where our beasts are
>To look if they be hungry or full.   310

CAIN:

>No, no, abide! We have a crow to pull.
>Hark, speak with me ere thou go.
>What? Thinkst thou to 'scape so?
>Wei! No! Thou gave me a foul despite
>And now is time that I requite.

ABEL:

>Brother, why art thou so to me in ire?

CAIN:

>Wei! Why was thy tenth so bright in fire,
>Whereas mine only but smoked,
>Right as it would us both have choked?

ABEL:

>God's will I trow it were   320
>That mine did burn so clear.
>If thine smoked, am I to blame?

CAIN:

>Why, yea! And thou shall pay the same.
>With cheek-bone, ere my hand I stay,
>Shall I have torn thy life away.

>CAIN *strikes* ABEL *with a jaw-bone;* ABEL *falls.*

>So lie down there and take thy rest;
>Thus loud-mouths get chastiséd best.

ABEL:

> Vengeance, vengeance, Lord, I cry!
> For I am slain, and not guilty. ABEL *dies.*

CAIN:

> Yea, lie there, old shrew! Lie there, lie!   330
> (*To the audience*)
> And if any of you think I did amiss,
> I shall it amend worse than it is,
> > That all men may it see.
> Well worse than it is,
> > Right so shall it be.

> But now, since he is brought to sleep,
> Into some hole fain would I creep.
> For fear I quake, and counsel need;
> If I be taken, I am good as dead.
> Here will I lie for forty days,   340
> And cursed be him that me first raise.

> *Enter* GOD *above.*

GOD:

> Cain! Cain!

CAIN:

> > Who is that that calls me?
> I am here, mayest thou not see?

GOD:

> Cain, where is thy brother Abel?

CAIN:

> Why ask of me? I think in hell,
> In hell I think he be —
> Whoso were there, might him see.
> Or somewhere he may be sleeping.
> When was he in my keeping?

GOD:

> Cain, Cain, thou art wild and mad: 350
> The voice of thy brother's blood
> That thou has slain in false wise,
> From earth to heaven for vengeance cries.
> And, for thou hast brought thy brother down,
> Here I give thee malediction.

GOD *makes a mark on* CAIN's *forehead.*

CAIN:
>Yea, deal out dole, for I will none,
>Or take it Thyself when I am gone.
>Since I have done such mickle sin
>That I may not Thy mercy win
>And Thou thus puts me from Thy grace,   360
>I shall hide me from Thy face,
>And whereso'er a man may find me,
>Let him slay me certainly,
>And whereso'er a man may me meet,
>Either by path or yet by street.
>And certainly when I am dead
>Bury me in Goodbower at the quarry's head.
>But from this place if I may part
>For all men give I not a fart.

GOD:
>Nay, Cain, that is not My will: 370
>I say that no man other kill.
>For he that slays thee, young or old,
>It shall be punished sevenfold. GOD *withdraws.*

CAIN:
>No matter! I wot whither I shall.
>In hell, I wot, must be my stall.
>It is no use mercy to crave;
>For if I pray, none must I have.
>
>But this corpse I wish were hid,
>>For some one might it find again:
>"Fly, false villain!" would he bid,   380
>>And ween I had my brother slain.
>
>But were Pickharness, my knave, here,
>We should bury him together.
>
>Ho, Pickharness! Scapethrift, ho! Pickharness, ho!

Enter PICKHARNESS.

PICKHARNESS:
>Master! Master!

CAIN:

>Hear'st thou, boy? There is a pudding in the pot.
>Take thee that, boy, take thee that! *Strikes him.*

PICKHARNESS:

>I curse thy pate under thy hood,
>Though thou were father of my blood!
>All day long I run and trot,   390
>>And thou do strike without an end;
>Thus does it come that buffets I got.

CAIN:

>>Peace, man! I did it but to use my hand.

>But hark, boy, I have a counsel to thee to say:
>I slew my brother this same day.
>I pray thee, good boy, if thou may,
>>To run away with his bone.

PICKHARNESS:

>Wei! Out upon thee, thief!
>>Has thou thy brother slain?

CAIN:

>>Peace, man, for God's pain!   400

>I said it all askance.

PICKHARNESS:

>Yea, but for dread and grievance,
>>Here I thee forsake.
>We must have a mickle mischance
>>If the bailiffs us take.

CAIN:

>Ah, sir, I cry you mercy! Cease,
>And I shall give you free release.

PICKHARNESS:

>What, wilt thou cry my peace
>>Throughout this land? *He indicates the audience.*

CAIN:

>Yea, that I vow to God at once.   410

PICKHARNESS:

How e'er thou do, may you never thrive.

CAIN:

Stand up, my good boy, now at once,
And bid all peace, both man and wife,
And whoso does as pleases me
Full smooth in fortune shall he be.
But thou must be my good boy,
And cry "Oyes, oyes, oy!"

PICKHARNESS:

Oh yes, oh yes, here's thy boy!

He climbs up, calling for silence, and CAIN *follows him to make a proclamation in the King's name.* PICKHARNESS *comes down from the rostrum to add his own comments to the audience.*

CAIN:

I command you all in the king's name. . . .

PICKHARNESS:

And in my master's, false Cain.   420

CAIN:

That no man with them find fault or blame. . . .

PICKHARNESS:

Yea, cold fare is at my master's home.

CAIN:

Neither with him nor with his knave. . . .

PICKHARNESS:

Why now I think my master does rave.

CAIN:

For they are true, so all men hold. . . .

PICKHARNESS:

My master sups no cawl but cold. . . .

CAIN:

The king writes to you his will.

PICKHARNESS:

Yet ate I never half my fill.

CAIN:

> The king commands that they be safe. . . .

PICKHARNESS:

> Yea, a draught of drink fain would I have. . . .   430

CAIN:

> At their own will, let them wander. . . .

PICKHARNESS:

> My stomach is ready to surrender.

CAIN:

> Look no man reproach them, one or other. . . .

PICKHARNESS:

> This same is he that slew his brother.

CAIN:

> Bid all men give them love devout. *He descends.*

PICKHARNESS:

> Yea, ill-spun cloth comes foully out.

CAIN (*Aside to* PICKHARNESS):

> Ill may you prosper if thou go thus about!
> (*To the audience.*)
> Bid every man their reward to pay.

PICKHARNESS:

> Yea, give Dun, thine horse, a wisp of hay!

CAIN:

> Wei! Come down in the devil's way!   440

> PICKHARNESS *has climbed up out of* CAIN'*s reach.*

>> I hope the devil may thee catch;
> For but it were Abel, my brother,
>> Till now I never knew thy match.

PICKHARNESS (*To the audience*):

> Now old and young, ere that ye wend,
> The same blessing withouten end,
>> Altogether shall ye have,
> That the God of heaven my master does give.
> Enjoy it well, whiles that ye live;
>> May He well it vouchsafe.

CAIN:

> Come down again, in the devil's way,   450
> > And anger me no more!

> PICKHARNESS *climbs down and obeys* CAIN's *commands*
> *silently, fetching the plough and team.*

> And take yon plough, I say,
> > And wend thee forth fast before;
> And I shall, if I may,
> > Teach thee another lore.
> I warn thee, lad, for aye,
> > From henceforth ever more,
> That thou do grieve me nought.
> For, by God's sides, and if thou do,
> I shall hang thee up on this plough   460
> With this rope, lo, lad, lo!
> By Him that me dear bought. *Exit* PICKHARNESS *and team.*

> (*To the audience*)
> Now farewell, fellows all, for I must needs off-wend,
> And to the devil be in thrall, world without all end:
> Ordained already is my stall, down there with the fiend.
> Forever ill may him befall, that thither me commend
> > This tide,
> Farewell less, and farewell more!
> For now and ever more
> > I will go me to hide. *Exit.*   470

Characters
NOAH
GOD
WIFE TO NOAH
1ST SON
2ND SON
3RD SON
1ST WIFE
2ND WIFE
3RD WIFE

The RAVEN ⎫ these could be mechanical devices or
Two DOVES ⎭ impersonations by actors

When Noah, in his first speech, describes the wickedness of men, a parade or dance of the Seven Deadly Sins could accompany his words (see lines 51–4, especially). It could continue during God's speech from above; as God descends, the acting area would clear of all except Noah.

Staging
An upper level is required for GOD's first appearance, and a small hill on which Noah's WIFE can sit and spin.

The Ark is probably carried into the acting area and quickly assembled (as by divine help and, possibly, to music); it can then be loaded with cattle and possessions by the three SONS and their WIVES. It may be wheeled off before the end of the play.

II Noah and His Sons

Enter NOAH.

NOAH:
    Mightfull God in *verité*,   maker of all that is,
    Three Persons withouten nay,   one God in endless bliss,
    Thou made both night and day,   beast, fowl, and fish,
    All creatures that live may   wrought Thou at Thy wish,
          As Thou well might:
    The sun, the moon, *verément*,
    Thou made, the firmament,
    The stars also, full fervent
          To shine, Thou made full bright.

    Angels Thou made full even,   each order that is,   10
    To have Thy bliss in heaven;   this did Thou more and less,
    Full marvellous to namen.   Yet was their unkindness
    More by seven times seven   than I can well express.
          For why?
    Of all angels in brightness
    God gave Lucifer most lightness,
    Yet proudly he flit his dais,
          And set him even Him by.

    He thought himself as worthy   as Him that him made
    In brightness, in beauty: therefore He did him degrade,   20
    Put him in low degree   soon after — quick as said —
    Him and all his meney,   where he may be unglad
          For ever.
    Never shall they win away
    Hence, until doomsday,
    But burn in bale for aye;
          They shall never dissever.

Soon after, that gracious Lord   in His likeness made man,
That place to be re-stored,   even as He began.
Of the Trinity by accord,   Adam, and Eve that woman,   30
To multiply without discord   in paradise put He them;
        And then to both
Gave in commandment
On the Tree of Life to lay no hand.
But yet the false fiend
        Made Him with man wroth.

Enticed man to gluttony,   stirred him to sin in pride.
But in paradise, surely,   might no sin abide;
And therefore man full hastily   was put out in that tide
In woe and wretchedness to be,   and pains deep-tried   40
        To know:
First on earth, and then in hell
With fiends for to dwell;
Unless He His mercy deal
        To those that will Him trow.

Oil of mercy He us hight,   as I have heard read,
To every living wight   that would love Him and dread;
But now, before his sight,   every living head,
Most part of day and night,   sin in word and deed
        Full bold: 50
Some in pride, ire, and envy,
Some in covetous and gluttony,
Some in sloth and lechery,
        And otherwise, manyfold.

Therefore I dread lest God   on us will take vengeance;
For sin is now abroad,   without any repentance.
Six hundred years and odd   have I, without distance,
On earth, as any sod,   lived with great grievance
        Alway;
And now I wax old,   60
Sick, sorry, and cold;
As muck upon mould
        I widder away.

But yet will I cry   for mercy, and call.
Noah, Thy servant, am I,   Lord over all!
Therefore me — and my fry   that shall with me fall —
Save from villainy,   and bring to Thy hall
      On high;
And keep me from sin
This world within.   70
Come King of Mankind,
      I pray Thee hear my cry.

Enter GOD *above.*

GOD:

Since I have made all thing   that is living,
Duke, emperor, and king,   with Mine own hand,
For to have their liking   by sea and by sand,
Every man to My biding   should be bound
      Full fervent,
That made man such a creature,
Fairest of favour.
Man must love Me *paramour* —   80
      In reason — and repent.

Methought I showed man love   when I made him to be
All angels above,   like to the Trinity;
And now in great reproof   full low lies he,
On earth himself to stuff   with sins that displease me
      Most of all.
Vengeance will I take
On earth, for sin sake;
My anger thus will I wake
      Both to great and to small.   90

I repent full sore   that ever made I man;
By Me he sets no store,   and I am his sovereign.
I will destroy therefore   both beast, man, and woman:
All shall perish, less and more.   Their bargain may they ban
      That ill did do.
On earth I see right nought
But sin that is unsought;
Of those that well ha' wrought
      Find I but a few.

Therefore shall I fordo   all this middle-world   100
With floods that shall flow   and roar hideous abroad.
I have good cause thereto;   of me no man's afeard.
As I say, so shall I do: for vengeance draw my sword,
          And make end
Of all that bear a life,
Save Noah and his wife,
For they would never strife
          With Me, nor Me offend.

To his own mickle win,   hastily will I go
To Noah my servant, to begin,   to warn him of his woe.   110
On earth I see but sin   reigning to and fro
Among both more and min,   each one t'other foe
          With all their intent.
All shall I fordo
With floods that shall flow;
Work shall I to their woe
          That will not repent.

GOD *descends to address* NOAH.

Noah, My friend, I thee command,   from sorrows thee to shield,
A ship that thou should frame   of nail and board full well.
Thou alway was a good workman,   to Me as true as steel,   120
To My bidding obedient;   friendship shall thou feel
          As thy reward.
In length thy ship should be
Three hundred cubits, warn I thee;
In height even thirty,
          Of fifty also broad.

Annoint thy ship with pitch and tar,   without as well within,
The water to forbear: this is a noble doing.
Look no man thee should mar.   Three tiers of decks begin:
Thou must spend many a spar   before this work thou win   130
          To t'end fully.
Make in thy ship also,
Parlors one or two,
And stables many more
          For the beasts that there must be.

One cubit in height   a window shall thou make;
At the side a door, with sleight,   beneath it shall thou take.
With thee shall no man fight,   nor do thee any wreak.
When all is done thus right,   thy wife, that is thy mate,
     Take in to thee;   140
Thy sons of good fame,
Shem, Japhet and Ham,
Take in also them,
       And their wives also three.

For all shall be fordone   that live on land, but ye,
With floods that from above   shall fall, and in plenty.
It shall begin full soon   to rain uncessantly,
After days seven be done,   and endure for days forty,
     Withouten fail.
Take to thy ship also   150
Of each kind beastis two,
Male and female − but no more −
     Ere thou pull up thy sail

For they may thee avail   when all this thing is wrought.
Stuff thy ship with victual,   so from hunger ye perish not.
As to beasts, birds and cattle − for them have thou in thought −
For them is My counsel   that some succour must be sought
     In haste;
They must have corn and hay
And other food alway.   160
Do now as I thee say,
     In the name of the Holy Ghost.

NOAH:

Ah, *Benedicité*! What art Thou that thus
Tells me before that which shall be?   Thou art full marvellous:
Tell me, for charity,   thy name so gracious.

GOD:

My name is of dignity,   and also full glorious
     To know:
I am God most mighty:
One God, in Trinity,
Made thee and ev'ry man to be;   170
     To love Me well thou owe.

NOAH:

> I thank Thee, Lord so dear,   that would vouchsafe
> Thus low to appear,   to a simple knave.
> Bless us, Lord, here,   for charity I it crave;
> The better may we steer   the ship that we shall have,
>> Certain.

GOD:

> Noah, to thee and to thy fry
> My blessing grant I;
> Ye shall wax and multiply
>> And fill the earth again.   180

> When all these floods are past   and fully gone away. *Exit* GOD.

NOAH:

> Lord, homeward will I haste   as fast as that I may;
> My wife will I ask   what she wills to say;
> And I am aghast   that we get some fray
>> Betwixt us both,
> For she bites sharply;
> For little's oft angry.
> If anything wrong be,
>> Soon is she wroth. *He goes to his* WIFE.

> (*To his* WIFE)
> God speed, dear wife!   How fare ye?   190

WIFE:

> Now, as ever might I thrive,   the worse that I thee see.
> Do tell me in brief   where did thou thus long be?
> To death may we drive,   for all it means to thee,
>> For want.
> While we sweat and swink,
> Thou does just as thou think;
> Yet of meat and of drink
>> Have we real skant.

NOAH:

> Wife, we are hard stead   with tidings anew.

WIFE:

> But thou were worthy be clad   in Stafford blue,   200

For that art alway afraid,   be it false or true.
But God knows I am treated —   and that may I rue —
      Full ill;
I trust from thee may borrow,
From evening until morrow
Thou speakst ever of sorrow.
         God send thee once thy fill.

(*To the women in the audience*)
We women must harry   all ill husbands.
I have one — by Mary   that loosed me from my bands! —
If he be troubled, I must tarry,   howsoever it stands,   210
With semblance full sorry,   and wring both my hands
      For fear.
But still, otherwhile,
What with game and with guile,
I shall smite and smile,
        And pay him back dear.

NOAH:
Wei! Hold thy tongue, ram-skyte,   or I shall thee still.

WIFE:
By my thrift, if thou smite,   turn on thee I will.

NOAH:
We shall assay ye as tight.   Have at thee, Gill!
Upon the bone shall it bite. *He strikes her.*

WIFE:
                  Ah, so! Mary, thou smitest ill!   220
      But I suppose
I shall not in thy debt
From this floor now flit:
Take thee there a langett
      To tie up thy hose! *She strikes him.*

NOAH:
Ah! Wilt thou so?   Mary, that is mine!

WIFE:
Thou shall ha' three for two,   I swear by God's pain!

NOAH:

> And I shall quite thee those,   in faith or in sin.

WIFE:

> Out upon thee, ho!

NOAH:

> > > Thou can both bite and whine;
> > And thou roared.   230
> *(To the audience.)*
> For all if she strike,
> She will furious shriek;
> In faith, I hold none her like
> > In all middle-world.

> But I will keep charity,   for I have much to do.

WIFE:

> Here shall no man tarry thee;   I pray thee to go!
> Full well may we miss thee,   as ever have I rue.
> To spin will I set me. *She sits down to spin.*

NOAH:

> > > Wei! Farewell, lo!
> > But, wife,
> Pray for me busily,   240
> Till after I come to thee.

WIFE:

> Even as thou pray'st for me,
> > As ever might I thrive.

NOAH:

> I tarry full long   from my work, I trow;
> Now my gear will I bring,   and thitherward draw.

He goes to build his ship.

> Full ill is my going,   the sooth for to know;
> But if God guard me from wrong,   I dare well be a daw
> > In man's ken.
> Now assay will I
> What I know of shipwrightry   250
> *In nomine Patris, et Fillii,*
> > *Et Spiritus Sancti. Amen.*

To begin with this tree   my bones will I bend;
I trust that the Trinity   succour will send.
It fares full fair, think me,   this work to my hand.
Now blessed be He   that this did amend.
      Lo, here the length,
Three hundred cubits evenly;
Of breadth, lo, is it fifty;
The height is even thirty   260
      Cubits, full strength.

Now my gown will I cast,   and work in my coat;
Make will I the mast   ere I flit one foot.
Ah! My back, I trow, will burst!   This is a sorry note!
It is wonder that I last: I am such an old dote,
      All dold,
To begin such a work.
My bones are so stark:
No wonder if they ache,
      For I am full old.   270

The mast-head and sail   both will I make;
The helm and the castle   also will I take;
To drive in each nail   will I not forsake.
This work can never fail,   that dare I undertake
      At once.
This is a fine engine:
These nails they so run
Thorough more and min,
      These boards every one.

Window and door,   even as he said;   280
Three sets of floor,   they are well made;
Pitch and tar full sure   thereupon laid.
This will ever endure;   therewith I am pleased.
      For why?
It is better wrought
Than I could have thought.
Him that made all of nought
      I thank only.

He goes to his WIFE, *his* SONS *and their* WIVES.

Now will I hie me,   and nought can I dither
My wife and my meiney   to bring even hither.   290
Attend here, and tidely,   wife; and consider
Hence must we flee,   all now together,
     In haste.

WIFE:

Why, sir, what ails you?
Who is't that assails you?
To flee it avails you
     If ye be aghast.

NOAH:

There is yarn on the reel   other, my dame.

WIFE:

Tell me all in detail,   or else get ye blame.

NOAH:

He, that sorrows can still   — blesséd be His name! —   300
He has behest, for our weal,   to shield us from shame,
     And said
All this world about,
With floods so stout
That shall run in a rout,
     Shall be overlaid.

He said all shall be slain,   except only we,
Our bairns that obey,   and their wives all three.
A ship he bad me ordain,   to save us and our fee;
Therefore with all our main   thank we that Lord free,   310
     The bater of bale.
Hie us fast! Go we hither.

WIFE:

I wot never whither;
I daze and I dither
     For fear of that tale.

NOAH:

Be not afeard. Have done;   truss up all our gear,
So we be there ere noon   and nothing more fear.

1ST SON:

    It shall be done full soon.   Brother help to bear.

2ND SON:

    Long I shall not be alone   to do my *devoir*,
          Brother Shem.   320

3RD SON:

    Without any yelp,
    In my might shall I help.

WIFE:

    Yes, for dread of a skelp,
          Help well thy dam!

    They go to the Ark, and all but the WIFE *go aboard.*

NOAH:

    Now are we there   as we should be.
    Do get in our gear,   our cattle and fee,
    Into this vessel here,   my children free.

WIFE:

    I was never barred-up ere —   as ever might I thee —
          In such a hostel as this!
    In faith, I cannot find   330
    Which is before, which is behind.
    But shall we here be penned,
          Noah, as have thou bliss?

NOAH:

    Dame, as it is skill,   here must we abide grace.
    Therefore, wife, with good will   come into this place.

WIFE:

    Sir, for neither Jack nor Gill,   will I turn my face
    Till I have on this hill   spun for a space
          On my distaff.
    Well were he that might get me!
    Now will I down here set me; *She sits down to spin.*   340
    And reed I no man prevent me,
          For dread of a sudden cuff.

NOAH (*Speaks from the Ark*):

    Look to the heaven!   The cateracts all,
    They are open full even,   great ones and small,
    And the planets there seven   left have their stall.
    These thunders and lightning   down here make fall
        Full stout
    Both high halls and bowers,
    Castles and towers.
    Full sharp are these showers   350
        That reign all about.

    Therefore, wife, have done;   come into ship fast.

WIFE:

    Aye, Noah, go clout thy shoon!   The better will they last.

1ST WIFE:

    Good Mother, come in soon,   for all is overcast,
    Both the sun and the moon.

2ND WIFE:

                       And many wind-blast
        Full sharp;
    These floods so strong run.
    Therefore, Mother, come in.

WIFE:

    In faith, yet will I spin;
        All in vain ye carp.   360

3RD WIFE:

    If ye like ye may spin,   Mother, in the ship.

NOAH:

    Now is this twice: come in,   dame, on my friendship.

WIFE:

    Whether I lose or I win,   in faith, thy fellowship,
    Set I not at a pin.   This spindle will I slip
        Upon this hill
    Ere I stir once a foot.

NOAH:

    Peter! I trow that we dote.
    Without any more note,
        Come in if ye will.

WIFE:

    Aye, the water nighs so near   that I sit not dry;   370

    Into ship with a fleer,   therefore, will I hie

    For dread that I drown here. *She hurries to the Ark.*

NOAH:

                       Dame, surely,

    It be'st bought full dear   ye abode so long near-by

            Out of ship.

WIFE:

    I will not, for thy bidding,

    Go from door to the midden.

NOAH:

    In faith, and for your long tarrying

           Ye shall have lick of the whip.

WIFE:

    Spare me not, I pray thee,   but do just as thou think;

    These great words shall not 'fray me.

NOAH:

                   Abide there, dame, and drink,   380

    For beaten shall thou be   with this staff till thou stink.

    Are the strokes good? Say me. *He threatens her.*

WIFE:

                 What say ye, Wat Wynk?

NOAH:

       Speak!

    Cry me mercy, I say!

WIFE:

    Thereto say I nay.

NOAH:

    Unless thou do, by this day,

           Thy head shall I break. *He threatens her again.*

WIFE (*To women in the audience*):

    Lord, I were at ease,   and in heart quite whole,

    Might I once have a mess   of widdow's cawl.

    (*To* NOAH)

    For *thy* soul, without lies,   should I deal penny dole: 390

So would more, and no fuss,   that I see in this hall
       Among wives that are here,
For the life that they lead,
Wish their husbands were dead;
(*To the audience*)
For, as ever eat I bread
       So wish I our sire were!

NOAH (*To men in the audience*):
    Ye men that have wives,   whiles they are young,
    If ye love your own lives,   chastise their tongue.
    Methink my heart rives —   and both liver and lung —
    To see such-like strifes   wedded-men among.   400
        But I,
    So may I have bliss,
    Shall chastise this.

WIFE:
    Yet may ye miss,
        Nichol Neddy!

NOAH:
    I shall make thee still as stone,   beginner of blunder!
    I shall beat thy back and bone,   and break all in sunder.
                         They fight.

WIFE:
    Out, alas, I am gone!   Out upon thee, man's wonder!

NOAH:
    See how she can groan,   and I lie under!
        But, wife,   410
    From this grip let us go,
    For my back is near in two.

WIFE:
    And I am beat so blue
        That I cannot thrive.

1ST SON:
    Ah, why fare ye thus,   Father and Mother, both?

2ND SON:
    Ye should not be so spitous,   standing so unsafe.

3RD SON:

    These weathers are so hideous,   with many a cold caught.

NOAH:

    We will do as ye bid us,   we will no more be wroth,

          Dear bairns. *He goes to steer the Ark.*

    Now to the helm will I hent,   420

    And to my ship attend.

WIFE:

    I see in the firmament,

          Methink, the seven stars.

NOAH:

    This is a great flood,   wife, take heed.

WIFE:

    So methought, as I stood.   We are in great dread;

    These waves are so wode.

NOAH:

                  Help, God, in this need!

    As Thou art steersman good,   and the best, as I reed,

          Of all,

    Thou rule us in this race,

    As Thou did me promise.   430

WIFE:

    This is a perilous case.

          Help, God, when we call!

The storm rages; the Ark tosses to and fro; time passes.

NOAH:

    Wife, attend the steer-tree,   and I shall assay

    The deepness of the sea   that we bear, if I may.

WIFE:

    That shall I do full wisely.   Now go thy way,

    For upon this flood have we   floated many day

          With pain. *He lowers plummet.*

NOAH:

    Now the water will I sound:

    Ah! It is far to the ground.

(*To the audience*)
This travail I expound,   440
       Have I spent in vain.

Above all the hills be seen   the water is risen late
Cubits fifteen.   But in a higher state
It may not be, I ween,   for this well I wit:
This forty days has rain been;   it will therefore abate,
       As God did reveal.
This water in haste
Again will I taste;   *He lowers plummet again.*
Now am I aghast —
       It is waned a great deal!   450

Now are the weathers ceased,   and cataracts up-knit,
Both the most and the least.

WIFE:

                    Methink, by my wit,
The sun shines in the east.   Lo, is not yond it?
We should have a good feast,   were these floods flit
       So spitous.

NOAH:

       We have been here, all we,
       Three hundred days and fifty.

WIFE:

       Aye, now wanes the sea;
          Lord, well is us.

NOAH *takes out his plummet again.*

NOAH:

       The third time will I tender   what deepness we bear.   460

WIFE:

       How long shall thou linger?   Lay in thy line there.

NOAH:

       I may touch with my finger   the ground even here.

WIFE:

       Then begins to engender   to us merry cheer.
          But husband,
       What ground may this be?

NOAH:
>The hills of Armenie.

WIFE:
>Now blessed be He
>>That thus for us ordained!

NOAH:
>I see tops of the hills high,   many at a sight;
>Nothing to hinder me,   the weather is so bright.   470

WIFE:
>These are of mercy   tokens full right.

NOAH:
>Dame, therefore thou counsel me,   what fowl best might
>>Know how
>With flight of its wing,
>To bring without tarrying,
>Of mercy some tokening,
>>Either from north or from south.

>For this is the first day   of the tenth month.

WIFE:
>The raven, durst I lay,   will come again soon.
>As fast as thou may,   cast him forth — have done!   480

>NOAH *sends out the raven.*

>He may happen today   come again ere noon
>>Without delay.

NOAH:
>I will cast out also
>The doves, one or two.   NOAH *sends out the doves.*
>Go your way, go;
>>God send you some prey.

>Now are these fowls flown   to several country.
>Pray we fast each one,   kneeling on our knee,
>To Him that is alone,   worthiest of degree,
>That He will send anon   our fowls some fee   490
>>To glad us.

WIFE:

> They may not fail of land,
> The water is so waned.

NOAH:

> Thank we God, all dominant,
>> That Lord that made us.

> It is a wonder-thing,   methink, soothly,
> They are so long tarrying,   the fowls that we
> Cast out in the morning.

WIFE:

>> Sir, it may be
> They tarry till they bring . . .

NOAH:

>> The raven is a-hungry
> Alway.   500
> He is without any reason:
> If he find any carrion,
> As peradventure be found,
>> He will not come away.

> The dove is more gentle: I give trust her unto;
> Like to the turtle,   for aye she is true.

WIFE:

> Hence in just a little,   she is coming: lew! lew!
> She is bringing in her bill   some tidings new
>> Behold!
> It is of an olive-tree   510
> A branch, it seems to me.

NOAH:

> It is sooth, perdy;
>> Right so is it called.

> Dove, bird fully blest,   fair may thee befall!
> Thou art true to thy tryst,   as stone in the wall.
> Full well I it wist   thou'd come back to thy hall.

WIFE:

> A true token is't   we shall savéd be all,
>> For why?

The water, since she come
Of deepness to plumb   520
Is fallen to a fathom
   And more certainly.

1ST SON:

 These floods are all gone,   Father, behold!

2ND SON:

 There is left right none,   of that be ye bold.

3RD SON:

 As still as a stone   our ship is stalled.

NOAH:

 Upon land here, at one,   that we were, fain I would.
   My children dear,
 Shem, Japhet and Ham,
 With glee and with game,
 Come go we, all the same;   530
   We will no longer abide here. *They all leave the Ark.*

WIFE:

 Here have we been,   Noah, long enough
 With trouble and teen,   and endured mickle woe.

NOAH:

 Look here on this green!   Neither cart nor plough
 Is left, as I ween,   neither tree nor bough,
   Nor other thing,
 But all is away;
 Many castles, I say,
 Great towns of array,
   Flung down has this flooding.   540

WIFE:

 These floods, that took no fright,   all this world so wide
 Have removed with their might,   by sea and by side.

NOAH:

 To death are they dight,   the proudest in pride
 Each and every wight   that ever was spied
   With sin:

All are they slain
And put unto pain.

WIFE:

From thence again
    May they never win?

NOAH:

Win? No, iwis.   But He, that might has,   550
Would have mind of their miss,   and admit them to grace.
As He in bale brings bliss,   I pray Him in this space,
In heaven high, with His,   to provide us a place,
        That we
With His saints in sight
And His angels bright,
May come to His light.
        Amen, for charity. *Exeunt.*

Characters
1ST SHEPHERD (Gyb)
2ND SHEPHERD (John Horn)
3RD SHEPHERD (Slow-Pace)
JACK GARCIO
ANGEL
MARY
CHRIST-CHILD

The ANGEL can be accompanied by a choir of angels.

Staging
An open area, surrounded by the audience is used for the fields.
The luxurious food which the shepherds describe is imaginary,
like their sheep; but some bread and, at least, two bottles of ale
should be brought on stage in the shepherds' *mails* or bags.

At one end of the acting area is the stable of Bethlehem.
The ANGEL appears at a higher level, as a bright light illuminates
the whole acting area. When he has gone, a star appears overhead
and should, if possible, move until it is directly above the stable.

III The First Shepherds' Play

Enter 1ST SHEPHERD *in very worn and poor clothes.*

1ST SHEPHERD:
    Ah, Lord, they are well   that from hence are past!
    For they do not feel   them too far down-cast.
    Here is mickle ill   and long has it last:
    Now in health and in weal;   now in wet and in blast;
        Now in care,
    Now in comfort again;
    Now is fair, now is rain;
    Now in heart full fain,
        And after full sore.

    Thus this world, as I say,   fares on each side,   10
    For after our play   with sorrows we're tried;
    For he that most may   when he sits in his pride,
    When it comes to assay   is casten down wide.
        This is seen:
    When richest is he,
    Then comes poverty;
    Horseman Jack Plenty
        Walks then, I ween.

    For this I thank God —   hark ye what I mean —
    That for even or odd   I have mickle teen;   20
    As heavy as a sod,   I weep with mine eyen,
    When I nap on my tod,   for care that has been
        And sorrow.
    All my sheep are gone;
    I am not left one,
    The rot has them slain.
        Now beg I and borrow.

My hands may I wring   and mourning make,
Unless good will spring   this land I'll forsake:
Rent and taxes are rising   and my purse is but weak;   30
I have nearly nothing   to pay or to take.
            I may sing
With purse penniless
That makes all this heaviness:
"Woe is me, in distress!" --
            There is no helping.

Thus set I my mind,   truly for to namen,
By my wit to find   how the dice can helpen.
My sheep are behind   fallen dead of the murrain;
If such ill luck me grind,   may God from his heaven   40
            Send grace!
To the fair will I
Some sheep for to buy
So I may still multiply,
            Despite my hard case.

Enter 2ND SHEPHERD *who does not see the* 1ST
SHEPHERD, *but addresses the audience.*

2ND SHEPHERD:
    Ben'dic'té, Ben'dic'té,   be us among,
    And save all that I see   here in this throng!
    May He save you and me,   athwart and endlong —
    He who hung on a tree.   I say you no wrong:
            Christ save us   50
    From all mischiefs,
    From robbers and thiefs,
    From those mens' griefs
            That oft are against us.

    Both boasters and braggers   God keep us fro,
    That with their long daggers   do mickle woe;
    From all bill-hackers   with slash-knives that go.
    Such wryers and wranglers   go to and fro
            For to crake.
    Whoso do complain   60
    Were better be slain;
    Both plough and wain
            Amends will not make.

(*Indicating a wealthy young man – possibly from among
the audience*)
He will act as proud   as a lord he were,
With head held in a cloud   and tight-curled his hair;
He speaks out loud   and fiercely does dare –
I would not it have trowed,   so gorgeous is his gear
   As he glides.
I wot not the better,
Nor which is greater –   70
The man or the master;
   So stoutly he strides.

If he ask me for aught   that he wants for his pay,
Full dear be it bought   if I say nay.
But God that all wrought,   to thee now I say,
"Help, so they are brought   to a better way
   For sake of their souls;
And send them good mending
With a short ending;
And with Thee to be dwelling   80
   When Thou to them calls."

(*To* 1ST SHEPHERD)
Ho there Gib! Good morn!   Whither goes thou?
Thou goes over the corn!   Gyb, I say, Ho!

1ST SHEPHERD:
 Who is that? John Horn,   I make God avow!
 I speak not in scorn;   John, how fares thou?

2ND SHEPHERD:
   Ha, Hay!
 Are ye in this town?

1ST SHEPHERD:
 Yea by my crown!

2ND SHEPHERD:
 I thought by your gown
   This was your array.   90

1ST SHEPHERD:
 I am for ever such;   wot I never what it gars.
 In this realm is no match;   no shepherd fares worse.

2ND SHEPHERD:
>   Poor men live in the ditch   and oft-time that mars:
>   The world is such.   Also helpers
>>   Is none here.

1ST SHEPHERD:
>   It is said full rife,
>   "A man may not wive
>   And also thrive,
>>   And all in one year."

2ND SHEPHERD:
>   First must we creep   and afterwards go.   100

1ST SHEPHERD:
>   I go to buy sheep.

2ND SHEPHERD:
>>   Nay, not so!
>   What, dream ye or sleep?   Where should they go?
>   Here have thou no keep.

1ST SHEPHERD:
>>   Ah, good sir, ho!
>   Who am I?
>   I will pasture my fee
>   Wheresoever likes me;
>   Here shall thou them see.

2ND SHEPHERD:
>   Not so hardy!

>   Not one sheep-tail   shall thou bring hither.

1ST SHEPHERD:
>   I shall bring — no fail —   a hundred together.   110

2ND SHEPHERD:
>   What, dost thou ail?   Long'st thou go any-whither?

1ST SHEPHERD:
>   They shall come *sans* fail.   Go now bell-wether!
>>   *He drives imaginary sheep.*

2ND SHEPHERD:
>   I say, *tyr*!

1ST SHEPHERD:
>   I say, *tyr*, now again.
>   I say skip over the plain.

2ND SHEPHERD:
>   Be thou never so fain,
>   Tup, I say, *whyr*!

1ST SHEPHERD:
>   What, will thou not yet,   I say, let the sheep go?
>   *Whop*!

2ND SHEPHERD:
>   Abide yet!

1ST SHEPHERD:
>   Will thou do so?
>   Knave hence! I bid flit.   It's good that thou do,   120
>   Or I shall thee hit   on thy pate. — Lo,
>   Thou shall reel! *He threatens to strike.*
>   I say give the sheep space.

2ND SHEPHERD:
>   Sir, a little of your grace!
>   Here comes Slowpace
>   From the mill-wheel.

Enter 3RD SHEPHERD, *on a horse carrying a sack of meal.*

3RD SHEPHERD:
>   What ado, what ado   is this you between?
>   Good day thou, and thou.

1ST SHEPHERD:
>   Hark what I mean
>   Now to say:
>   I was bound to buy store,   130
>   With my sheep me before:
>   And he says not one hair
>   Shall pass this way.

>   But, although he were mad,   this way shall they go.

3RD SHEPHERD:
>   Yea, but tell me good,   where *are* your sheep, lo?

2ND SHEPHERD:

    Now, sir, by my hood,   I have seen no mo;
    Not since I here stood.

3RD SHEPHERD:

                  God give you woe
          And sorrow!
    Ye fish before the net,
    And strive in this set: 140
    Such fools never I met
          Either even or morrow.

    (*To the audience*)
    It is wonder to wit   where wit should be found.
    There are old rogues, yet   standing on this ground:
    These would by their wit   make a ship be drowned;
    He were well quit   who sold for a pound
          Such two.
    They fight and they fly
    For what never comes nigh.
    It is mad to bid "hie"   150
          To an egg ere it go.

    (*To the* SHEPHERDS)
    May you sooner lack all,   than sorrow, I pray!
    Ye take after Moll   that went the same way:
    Many sheep could she poll   and but one had for aye.
    But she fared full foul;   her pitcher, I say,
          Was broken.
    "Ho, God!" she said;
    But one sheep yet she had.
    The milk-pitcher was low laid;
          Smithereens were its token.   160

    But since ye are bare   of wisdom to know,
    Take heed how I fare   and learn of my law:
    Ye need not to care,   if ye follow my saw.
    Hold ye my mare.   Now this sack throw
          On my back,
    Whilst I, with my hand,
    Loose the sack-band.
    Come near and by-stand,
          Both Gyb and Jack. *He empties the sack over them.*

> Is not all shaken out,   and no meal is therein?   170

1ST SHEPHERD:
> Yea, that is no doubt.

3RD SHEPHERD:
>   So are your wits thin,
> If ye look well about,   both maximum and min.
> So go your wit out,   even as it came in.
>   Gather up
> And seek it again.

2ND SHEPHERD:
> Should we not be fain?
> He has told us full plain
>   Of wisdom to sup.

Enter JACK GARCIO.

JACK:
> Now God give you care,   fools, all the same!
> Saw I never none so fare   but the fools of Gotham.   180
> Woe is her that you bare!   Your sire and your dam,
> Had she brought forth a hare,   a sheep or a lamb,
>   Had been well.
> Of all the fools I can tell,
> From heaven unto hell,
> Ye three bear the bell:
>   God give you all ill.

1ST SHEPHERD:
> How pastures our fee?   Tell me, good Jacken.

JACK:
> They're in grass up to knee.

2ND SHEPHERD:
>   Fare fall thee!

JACK:
>   Amen.
> If ye will ye may see;   your beasts ye ken. *Exit* JACK. 190

1ST SHEPHERD:
> Sit we down all three,   and drink shall we then.

3RD SHEPHERD:
> Yea, turd!
> I would rather eat.
> What is drink without meat?
> Get meat, get
> > And set us a board;

> Then may we go dine,   our bellies to fill.

2ND SHEPHERD:
> We must wait and pine.

3RD SHEPHERD:
> > > By God, sir, I ne'er will!
> I am worthy the wine,   methink it good skill.
> I serve men in vain: I fare full ill   200
> > At your manger.

1ST SHEPHERD:
> Come on, let us eat!
> It is best to entreat.
> It would be defeat
> > To stand in thy danger.

> Thou has ever been curst   since we met together.

3RD SHEPHERD:
> Now in faith, if I durst,   ye are even my brother.

2ND SHEPHERD:
> Let us eat at the crib first,   despite one thing or other,
> That these words may be pursed;   and let us go fodder
> > Our munch-pins.   210
> Lay forth of our store:
> Lo, here brawn of a bore!

1ST SHEPHERD:
> Set mustard afore!
> > Our meal now begins.

> Here a foot of a cow   well sauced, I ween.
> The leg of a sow   that powdered has been,
> Two blood-puddings, I trow;   a liver sausage between:
> Do gladly, sirs, now —   my brothers, I mean.
> > With more:

Both beef, and mutton   220
Of an ewe that was rotten —
Good meat for a glutton! —
      Come eat of this store.

2ND SHEPHERD:

I have here in my mail   boiled meat and roast:
E'en a portion of ox-tail   that would not be lost.
Ha, ha! God hail!   I spare for no cost:
A good pie, ere we fail —   this is good for the frost
      Of a morning —
And two swine-groins,
All a hare but the loins.   230
We need have no spoons
      Here at our mangering.

3RD SHEPHERD:

Here is, for the record,   the leg of a goose
With chickens, on board: pork 'n partridge — to boast —
And a tart for a lord   — how think you this does? —
A calf-liver, scored   with crab-apple juice —
      A good sauce!
This is a *resoraté* *He speaks in a Frenchified way.*
To make a good *appeté.*

1ST SHEPHERD:

Ye speak very learnedly —   240
      I hear by your clause.

Could ye, by knowledge of clergy,   reach us a drink,
I should be the more merry —   ye wot what I think.

2ND SHEPHERD:

Have good ale of Healy!   Beware now, I give ye th' wink!
For if thou drink deeply   in thy poll will it sink.

1ST SHEPHERD:

      Aye, so!
This is cure for all bale,
Good wholesome ale. *He drinks.*

3RD SHEPHERD:

Ye hold long the scale:
      Now let me go too. *He drinks.*   250

2ND SHEPHERD:
    Beshrew those lips,   if thou leave me no part.

1ST SHEPHERD:
    By God, he but sips!   Beguiled thou art:
    Behold how he grips!   2ND SHEPHERD *snatches cup.*

2ND SHEPHERD:
                         I shrew you so smart —
    And me on my hips —   unless I gar it
          Grow less.
    (*To the cup*)
    Be thou wine, be thou ale,
    Unless my breath fail,
    I shall set thee a-sail:
          God send thee good pass.   *He drinks.*

3RD SHEPHERD:
    By my dam's soul, Alice,   it was deeply drunken!   260

1ST SHEPHERD (*Peering into cup*):
    Now as ever I have bliss,   to the bottom it is sunken.

2ND SHEPHERD:
    Yet a bottle here is —

3RD SHEPHERD:
                         That is well spoken;
    By my thrift, we must kiss!

2ND SHEPHERD:
                         — that had I forgotten.
          But hark!
    Whoso can best sing
    Shall have the beginning.

1ST SHEPHERD:
    Now praise at the parting:
          I shall set you a'work.

    He leads the others in a song.

1ST SHEPHERD:
    We have done our part   and sungen right well.
    I drink for my part.   *He drinks.*

2ND SHEPHERD:
>   Hold back: let the cup reel. *He drinks.* 270

1ST SHEPHERD:
> God forbid thou should spare't,   if thou drink every deal.

3RD SHEPHERD:
> Thou has drunken a quart;   therefore choke thee the devil.

1ST SHEPHERD:
>   Thou raves:
> And it were for a sow,
> There is drink enow.

3RD SHEPHERD (*Peering into the empty cup*):
> By the hands that it drained, now
>   Ye two be both knaves.

1ST SHEPHERD:
> Nay, we are knaves all: so think me best,
> Thus, sir, should ye call.

2ND SHEPHERD:
>   At that, let it rest:
> We want not to brawl.

1ST SHEPHERD:
>   Then would I we guess'd   280
> Who this meat shall   into panier cast.

3RD SHEPHERD:
>   Sirs, hear's:
> For our souls let us do
> And poor men give it to.

1ST SHEPHERD:
> Gather up, lo, lo!
>   Ye hungry beggars and friars!

2ND SHEPHERD:
> It draws near night.   Come, go we to rest.
> Indeed, I am ready dight: I think it the best.

3RD SHEPHERD:
> For fear we be fright,   a cross let us cast —

Christ-cross, *benedité*,   to east and to west —   290
    For dread.
Jesus o' *Nazarus*
Crucifixus;
Marcus, Andreus,
        God be our speed!   *The* SHEPHERDS *sleep.*

The ANGEL *enters above and sings.*

ANGEL:

Hark, herdsmen! Awake!   Give worship ye shall:
He is born for your sake,   Lord perpetual.
He is comen to take   and ransom you all;
Your sorrow to slake,   King Imperial,
        He behests.   300
That child is born
At Bethelem this morn:
Ye shall find him beforn,
        Betwixt two beasts.   *Exit* ANGEL.

1ST SHEPHERD:

Ah, God's dear *Dominus*!   What was that song?
It was wonder curious,   with small notes among.
I pray to God, save us   now in this throng!
I am 'feard, by Jesus,   somewhat be wrong.
        Methought
One screamed aloud.   310
I suppose it was a cloud;
In my ears it soughed,
        By Him that me bought!

2ND SHEPHERD:

Nay, that may not be,   I say you certain,
For he spake to us three   as he had been a man.
When he lightened this lea,   my heart shaked then:
An angel was he —   tell you I can —
        No doubt.
He spake of a bairn:
We must seek him, I warn: 320
That betokens yond starne
        That stands yonder out.   *He points to the sky.*

3RD SHEPHERD:

    It was a marvel to see,   so bright as it shon.

    It would have trowed, verily,   that thunder it flung:

    But I saw with mine eye   as I leaned on this stone.

    It was a merry glee;   such heard I never none.

        I record

    That he said in a scream —

    Or else I do dream —

    We should go to Beth'lem   330

        To worship that Lord.

1ST SHEPHERD:

    That same child is He   that prophets oft told

    Should make those free   that Adam had sold.

2ND SHEPHERD:

    Attend unto me!   This is enrolled

    By the words of Isay: "A Prince most bold

        Shall He be,

    And King with crown

    Sat on David's throne."

    Such was never none

        Seen with our eye.   340

3RD SHEPHERD:

    Also Isay says —   our fathers us told —

    That a virgin should pass   of Jesse, that would

    Bring forth, by grace,   a Flower so bold.

    That virgin now has   these words upheld,

        As ye see.

    Trust it now we may

    He is born this day:

    Exiet virga

        De radice Jesse.

1ST SHEPHERD:

    Of Him spake more: Sibyl, as I ween,   350

    And Nebuchadnezzar,   to our faith alien:

    In the fiery furnace there,   three children were seen,

    But a fourth stood before,   that God's Son might have been.

2ND SHEPHERD:
>   That figure
>   Was saying by revelation
>   That God would have a Son;
>   This is a good lesson
>   For us to consider.

3RD SHEPHERD:
>   Of Him spake Jeremy,   and Moses also
>   Where he saw, him by,   a burning bush — lo!   360
>   When he came to espy   if it were so,
>   Unburned was it truly   at coming thereto —
>   A wonder!

1ST SHEPHERD:
>   That was to let see
>   Her holy virginity;
>   That undefiled should she be —
>   Thus do I ponder —

>   And should have a child   such as never was seen.

2ND SHEPHERD:
>   Peace, man, thou art beguiled!   Thou shall see Him with eyen —
>   Of a maiden so mild   great marvel I mean;   370
>   Yea, and she undefiled,   a virgin clean —
>   And very soon.

1ST SHEPHERD:
>   Nothing is impossible,
>   In sooth, that God will;
>   It shall be so stable
>   That God will have done.

2ND SHEPHERD:
>   Habbakkuk and Ely   prophesied so,
>   Elizabeth and Zachary,   and many other mo;
>   And David as verily   is witness thereto,
>   John Baptist surely,   and Daniel also.   380

3RD SHEPHERD:
>   So saying,
>   He is God's Son alone;

Without Him shall be none;
His seat and His throne
      Shall be everlasting.

1ST SHEPHERD:
    Virgil in his poetry   said in his verse,
    Even thus very learnedly,   as I shall rehearse:
        Iam nova progenies caelo   demittitur alto;
        Iam redit et Virgo,   redeunt Saturnia regnam.

2ND SHEPHERD:
    Wei! Turd! What speak ye   here in my ears?   390
    Hold back the clergy!   You are one with the friars;
        So you do preach.
    It seems by your Latin
    You studied a lesson.

1ST SHEPHERD:
    Hark, sirs! Have done;
        I shall you teach.

    He said from heaven   a new kind is sent
    Whom they say a virgin,   our miss to amend,
    Shall conceive full even.   Thus make I an end.
    And yet more to namen,   I say Saturn shall bend   400
        Unto us,
    With peace and plenty,
    With riches and *meiney*,
    Good love and charity
        Blended amongst us.

3RD SHEPHERD:
    And I hold this true;   that there shall be,
    When that King comes new,   peace by land and by sea.

2ND SHEPHERD:
    Now brothers, adieu!   Take tent unto me:
    I would that we knew   this song so free
        Of the angel;   410
    I heard him tell open
    He was sent down from heaven.

1ST SHEPHERD:
> It is truth that ye namen:
>> I heard well his spell.

2ND SHEPHERD:
> Now, by God that me bought,   it was a merry song!
> I dare say that he brought   four and twenty to one long.

3RD SHEPHERD:
> I would it were sought,   that same, us among.

1ST SHEPHERD:
> In faith, I trow nought   so many he throng
>> On a heap:
> They were gentle and small,   420
> And well toned withal.

3RD SHEPHERD:
> Yea, but I know them all:
>> Now list I to't leap.

1ST SHEPHERD:
> Break out with your voice!   Let's see how ye yelp!

3RD SHEPHERD:
> I have cold in my nose: I must have some help.

2ND SHEPHERD:
> Ah, thy heart's in thy hose!

1ST SHEPHERD:
>>>> Now, I'll have your scalp,
> If this song you do lose!

3RD SHEPHERD:
>>>> Thou art an ill whelp,
>> In your anger!

2ND SHEPHERD:
> Go to now: begin!

1ST SHEPHERD:
> To the work he'll not run.   430

3RD SHEPHERD:
> God let us never have done!
>> Now take up my song.

He sings and the others soon join in.

1ST SHEPHERD:
Now an end have we done   of our song this tide.

2ND SHEPHERD:
Fair fall thy groan!   Well has thou hied.

3RD SHEPHERD:
Then forth let us run.   I will not abide.

1ST SHEPHERD:
No light makes the moon;   that have I espied.
        Never the less,
Let us hold our behest.

2ND SHEPHERD:
That hold I best.

3RD SHEPHERD:
Then must we go east,   440
        After my guess.

They go to Bethlehem.

1ST SHEPHERD:
Would God that we might   this young babe see.

2ND SHEPHERD:
Many prophets that sight   desired verily —
To have seen that bright.

3RD SHEPHERD:
              If God so high
Would show us that wight,   we might say, perdy,
        We had seen
What many saint desired,
And prophets inspired:
Of Him they enquired,
        Yet closed are their eyen.   450

2ND SHEPHERD:
God grant us that grace!

3RD SHEPHERD:
              God so do!

The star shines.

1ST SHEPHERD:

    Abide sirs, a space,   Lo, yonder, lo!
    It comes in a race,   yond star us to.

2ND SHEPHERD:

    It is a great blaze!   On our way let us go

    They arrive at the stable.

        Here He is.

3RD SHEPHERD:

    Who shall go in before?

1ST SHEPHERD:

    I not reck, by my hoar.

2ND SHEPHERD:

    Ye are of the old store;
        It befits you, iwis.

    They enter the stable, 1ST SHEPHERD *leading.*

1ST SHEPHERD:

    Hail, King I Thee call!   Hail Most of Might!   460
    Hail, the Worthiest of all!   Hail, Duke! Hail, Knight!
    Of great and small   Thou art Lord by right.
    Hail, Perpetual!   Hail fairest Wight!
        Here I offer:
    I pray Thee to take,
    If Thou would, for my sake —
    To play with, as Thou like —
        This little spruce coffer.

2ND SHEPHERD:

    Hail, little tiny Mop,   Rewarder of meed!
    Hail! But one drop   of grace at my need!   470
    Hail! little Milksop!   Hail, David's Seed!
    Of our creed Thou art crop.   Hail, in Godhead!
        This ball
    I would Thou receive!
    Little is that I have;
    This will I vouchsafe
        To play Thee withall.

3RD SHEPHERD:

    Hail, Maker of men!   Hail, Sweeting!

    Hail, as well as I can!   Hail, pretty Miting!

    I bow down to Thee then,   for gladness near weeping.   470

    Hail, Lord! Here I ordain,   now at our meeting,

        This bottle —

    It is an old byword,

    "It is a good sport

    To drink from a gourd" —

        It holds a full pottle.

MARY:

    He, that all mighty deeds may,   the Maker of heaven —

    That is for to say,   the Son I am given —

    Reward you this day   as He set all, in days seven:

    May He grant you for aye   His bliss full even   490

        Continuing,

    And give you good grace!

    Tell forth of this case;

    So He speed your pace

        And grant you good ending.

1ST SHEPHERD:

    Fare well, fair Lord,   and thy mother also.

2ND SHEPHERD:

    We shall this record   wherever we go.

3RD SHEPHERD:

    We must all be restored —   God grant it be so!

1ST SHEPHERD:

    Amen to that word!   Sing we thereto

        On height: 500

    To joy all the same,

    With mirth and game,

    To the laud of this Lamb

        Sing we in sight.   *Exeunt, singing.*

Characters
1ST SHEPHERD (Coll)
2ND SHEPHERD (Gyb)
3RD SHEPHERD (Daw)
MAK
WIFE OF MAK (Gill)
ANGEL
MARY
CHRIST-CHILD

The ANGEL can be accompanied by a choir of angels.

Staging
An open area, surrounded by the audience is used for the fields. To one side is Mak's cottage, which should have one or more doors, a cradle and a bed or settle on which Gill lies down; possibly there is a spinning-wheel and stool, and other household effects and furniture. This cottage could also serve for the stable at Bethlehem; alternatively the stable could be at the opposite side of the main acting area.

The ANGEL appears at a higher level, as a bright light illuminates the whole acting area; when he exits, a star shines from the same place.

IV The Second Shepherds' Play

(with the adventures of Mak, the Sheep-Stealer)

Enter 1ST SHEPHERD.

1ST SHEPHERD:

    Lord, how this weather is cold!　　And I am ill-wrapped.
    I am nearly struck dold,　　so long have I napped:
    My legs they do fold;　　my fingers are chapped.
    It is not as I would,　　for I am all lapped
        In sorrow.
    In storms and tempest,
    Now in th' east, now in the west,
    Woe is him that has never rest
        Midday or morrow!

    But we silly farm-hands　　that walk on the moor,　　　　　10
    In faith, we are near-hands　　turned out of door.
    No wonder, as it stands,　　if we be poor,
    For the tilth of our lands　　lies fallow as a floor,
        As ye ken.
    We are so ham-bound,
    Over-taxed and down-ground;
    We have no rights allowed
        By these gentry-men.

    Thus they reave us of our rest,　　our Lady them harry!
    These men that are lord-fast,　　they cause the plough tarry.　　20
    "That," men say, "is for the best!"　　We find it contrary!
    Thus are farm-hands oppressed,　　to the point they miscarry
        Alive.
    Thus the lords hold us under;
    Thus they bring us to blunder:
    It were a great wonder
        If e'er we should thrive.

There comes a lord's swain,   as proud as a po:
He must borrow my wain,   and my plough also —
Then I am full fain   to grant ere he go.   30
Thus live we in pain,   in anger and woe,
        By night and day.
He must have what he wanted
And I must foregang it;
I were better off hanged
        Than once say him nay.

For if man get braid on his sleeve,   or a badge, now-a-days,
Woe to him that him grieve   or that once gainsays.
None dare him reprove,   such mastery he sways;
Yet none may believe   one word that he says —   40
        No letter.
He can make purveyance
With boast and bragance;
And all is for maintenance
        Of men that are greater.

It does me good, as I walk   thus on mine own,
Of this world for to talk   in manner of moan.
To my sheep will I stalk,   and harken anon,
And there bide on a balk,   or sit on a stone
        Full soon;   50
For I trow, perdy,
True men if they be,
We get more company
        Ere it be noon.

Enter 2ND SHEPHERD, *not seeing the* 1ST.

2ND SHEPHERD:
    Ben'di'té and *Dominus*!   What may this all mean?
    Why fares the world thus?   Like have we not seen.
    Lord, this weather is spitous,   and the wind is full keen,
    And the frosts are so hideous   they water mine eyne —
        No lie.
    Now in dry, now in wet,   60
    Now in snow, now in sleet;
    When my shoes freeze to my feet
        It is not at all easy.

But as far as I ken,   or yet as I go,
We silly wedded men   endure mickle woe:
We have sorrow now and again;   it falls often so.
Silly Cappel, our hen,   both to and fro
   She cackles;
If begin she to croak,
To groan or to cluck,   70
Woe is't him is our cock,
   For he is in shackles!

These men that are wed   have not all their will;
When they are hard stead,   they sigh very still.
God wot they are led   full hard and full ill;
In bower or in bed   they say nought theretill.
   This tide
My place have I found;
I know my lesson:
Woe is him that is bound,   80
   For he must so abide.

But now late in our lives   — a marvel to me;
That I think my heart rives   such wonders to see:
That, as destiny drives,   it should so be —
Some men will have two wives,   and some men three
   In their store.
Some are woe that have any!
But so far can I see:
Woe is him that has many,
   For he feels it sore.   90

(*To young men in the audience.*)
But, young men a-wooing,   by God that you bought,
Be well ware of a wedding;   and think in your thought:
"Had-I-known" is a thing   that serves you for nought.
Much long-lasting wailing   has a wedding home-brought,
   And grief,
And many a sharp shower;
For ye may catch in an hour
What shall sting in thee full sour
   As long as ye live.

For, as e'er read I 'pistle,   I have one for my dear   100
As sharp as a thistle,   as rough as a briar;
She is browed like a bristle,   with sour-looking cheer;
Had she once wet her whistle,   she could sing full clear
                    Her *Paternoster.*
She is as great as a whale;
She has a gallon of gall.
By Him that died for us all,
           I wish I had run till I had lost her!

1ST SHEPHERD:
     God take care of us all!   Stone-deaf here ye stand.

2ND SHEPHERD:
     The devil in thy maw   for waiting around!   110
     Saw thou, anywhere, Daw?

1ST SHEPHERD:
                              Yea, on fallow-land
     Heard I him blow.   He is coming here at hand,
              Not far.
     Stand still.

2ND SHEPHERD:
                    Why?

1ST SHEPHERD:
     He is coming, hope I.

2ND SHEPHERD:
     He will tell us both a lie
              Unless we be ware.

Enter 3RD SHEPHERD, *a boy.*

3RD SHEPHERD:
     Christ's cross me speed,   and Saint Nicholas!
     Thereof had I need;   it is worse than it was.
     Whoso can take heed   and let the world pass,   120
     Sees it ever in dread   and brittle as glass;
              And it slithers.
     This world fared never so,
     With marvels moe and moe:
     Now in weal, now in woe,
              And everything flithers.

Was never since Noah's flood   such floods ever seen,
The winds and rains are so rude,   and storms all so keen:
Men stammered and stood   in doubt, as I ween.
Now God turn all to good!   I say as I mean,   130
      For ponder:
These floods do so drown,
Both in fields and in town,
And bear it all down:
      And that is a wonder.   *He sees the others.*

We that walk in the nights,   our cattle to keep,
We see sudden sights   when other men sleep.
Yet methink my heart lights: I see runagates peep.
Ye two are fierce wights —   I will give my sheep
      A turn.   140
But full ill have I meant:
As I walk on this bent,
I can lightly repent,
      My toes if I spurn.

(*To the others*)
Ah, sir, God you save,   and you, master mine!
A drink fain would I have,   and on somewhat to dine.

1ST SHEPHERD:
    Christ's curse, my knave,   thou art a lazy hind!

2ND SHEPHERD:
    How the boy loves to rave!   Wait for a later time:
      We have ate it.
    Ill luck on thy pate!   150
    Though the knave came late
    Yet is he in state
      To dine — if he had it.

3RD SHEPHERD:
    Such servants as I,   who do sweat and do swink,
    Eat our bread very dry;   and that's wrong as I think.
    We are oft wet and weary   and then master-man wink;
    Yet comes full lately   both dinner and drink.
      But safely
    Both our dame and our sire,
    When we have run in the mire,   160

They can cut down our hire
    And pay us full lately.

But hear my vow, master: as the fare you purvey,
Shall I do hereafter —   I'll work as you pay.
I shall do but little, sir,   and between times I'll play;
For my supper as yet never   heavy on stomach did lay
    In the field.
But why should I argue?
With my crook can I scarper:
And men say "Cheap bargain,   170
    Cheap and badly will yield."

1ST SHEPHERD:
Thou were an ill lad   to ride away wooing
With a man that had   but a little for spending.

2ND SHEPHERD:
Peace there, boy, I bad.   No more jangling,
Or I shall make thee full sad,   by the heaven's King!
    For thy pranks —
Where are our sheep, boy? — we scorn.

3RD SHEPHERD:
Sir, this same day at morn
I left them in the corn,
    When mattins they rang.   180

They have pasture good;   they cannot go wrong.

1ST SHEPHERD:
That is right. By the rood,   these nights are long!
Yet, I wish, ere we go,   someone gave us a song.

2ND SHEPHERD:
So *I* thought as I stood,   to cheer us along.

3RD SHEPHERD:
    I grant.

1ST SHEPHERD:
Let me sing the tenory.

2ND SHEPHERD:
And I the treble so high.

3RD SHEPHERD:

>Then the middle for me.
>>Let see how ye chant.   *Here they sing.*

>*Then enter* MAK, *with a cloak worn over his tunic.*

MAK:

>Now, Lord, by Thy names seven,   that made both moon
>>>>and starnes 190
>Many more than I can namen,   to me Thy will brings harms.
>I am all uneven   and troubled are my brains.
>Now would God I were in heaven,   for there do weep no bairns
>>Endlessly.

1ST SHEPHERD:

>Who is't that peeps so poor?

MAK:

>Would God ye wist how I fare!
>Lo, a man that walks on the moor,
>>And all unwillingly.

2ND SHEPHERD:

>Mak, where has thou gone?   Tell us tidings.

3RD SHEPHERD:

>Is *he* come? Then each one   take heed of his things.   200

>*He shakes* MAK'*s cloak to see what is hidden under it.*

MAK (*In a "posh" voice*):

>What! I be a yeoman,   I tell you, of the king's,
>The very selfsame one,   messenger of great lordings
>>And suchlike.
>Fie on you! Go off hence
>Out of my presence!
>I must have reverence.
>>Why, who is my like?

1ST SHEPHERD.

>Why make ye it so quaint?   Mak, ye do wrong.

2ND SHEPHERD:

>But, Mak, play ye the saint?   For that, I trow, ye long.

3RD SHEPHERD:
>   The knave can thus false words invent: the devil should
>   him hang.   210

MAK:
>   I shall make complaint;   and get you many a thwang
>   Without another word,
>   When I tell how ye doth.

1ST SHEPHERD:
>   But, Mak, is that the sooth?
>   Now take out that Southern tooth
>   And put in a turd.

2ND SHEPHERD:
>   Mak, the devil in your eye!   A blow will I lend you.

3RD SHEPHERD:
>   Mak, know ye not me?   By God, I too could teen you.

> *They are about to strike him.*

MAK:
>   God take care of you, all three!   Methought I had seen you.
>   Ye are a fair company.

1ST SHEPHERD:
>   You know us now, mean you?   220

2ND SHEPHERD.
>   Look out villain!
>   Thus late as thou goes,
>   What will men suppose?
>   I have heard ill news
>   Of sheep that be stolen.

MAK:
>   That I am true as steel,   all good men do wit.
>   But a sickness I feel,   that holds me full hot:
>   My belly fares not well: it is out of its state.

3RD SHEPHERD:
>   Seldom lies the devil   quite dead by the gate.

MAK:
>   Therefore   230
>   Full sore am I and ill,

If I stand stone-still.
I ate not a needle
    This month and more.

1ST SHEPHERD:
  How fares thy wife? By my hood   how does she do?

MAK:
  Lies waltering, by the rood,   by the fire, lo!
  And the house full of our brood.   She drinks well, too;
  Ill-speed all other good   that she wish to do!
      And so
  Eats as fast as she can   240
  And each year that comes to man
  She brings forth an infant,
      And some years two.

  But were I now more gracious   and richer by far,
  I were eaten out of house   and out of harbour.
  Yet is she a foul dowse,   if ye come near;
  There is no man trows   worse, or knows more
      Than ken I.
  Now will ye see what I proffer? —
  To give all in my coffer   250
  At tomorrow's mass to offer
      A penny, if only she would die.

2ND SHEPHERD:
  I wot so weary with waking   is none in this shire;
  I would sleep, were I taking   less to my hire.

3RD SHEPHERD:
  I am cold and am shaking,   and would have a fire.

1ST SHEPHERD:
  I am worn out with walking,   and deep in the mire —
      Keep awake you! *He lies down.*

2ND SHEPHERD:
  Nay, I will lie down by,
  For I must sleep, truly. *Lies down too.*

3RD SHEPHERD:
  As good a man's son was I   260
      As any of you.

He does the same, and makes MAK *do so.*

But Mak, come hither!   between us shall thou lie.

MAK:

Then might I hinder   the whispers you may try;
    So take heed.
From my top to my toe,
Manus tuas commendo,
Pontio Pilato!
    Christ's cross me speed.

The SHEPHERDS *sleep; and then* MAK *rises.*

Now were time for a man   that lacks what he would
To stalk privily then   unto a fold;   270
And nimbly to work then,   and be not too bold;
He'd pay dearly for the bargain,   if it were told
    At the ending.
Now were time for to reel:
But he needs good counsel
That fain would fare well,
    And has little for spending.

He casts a spell on the sleeping SHEPHERDS.

All about you a circle,   as round as the moon,
Till I have done what I will,   till that it be noon.
So lie ye there stone-still   until I have done.   280
And to that end I now tell   of good words a dozen:
    "On height
Over your heads my hand I lift:
Out go your eyes! Perish your sight!"
But still I must make better shift
    If it is to come right.   *The* SHEPHERDS *snore.*

Lord, how they sleep hard!   That may ye all hear.
I was never a shepherd,   but now will I learn.
If the flock be scared,   yet shall I nip near. *He goes to sheep.*
Ho! Draw hitherward!   Now mends all our cheer   290
    From sorrow,   *He has caught a sheep.*
A fat sheep, I dare say,
A good fleece, dare I lay.

Pay back when I may,
>   But this will I borrow. *He goes home with sheep.*

Ho! Gill, art thou in?   Get us some light.

WIFE:
>   Who makes such a din   this time of the night?
>   I am set for to spin;   think not I might
>   Rise a penny to win.   I curse them at height!
>   So fares   300
>   A housewife that has to be
>   Raised from her seat continually.
>   Here may no job be done featly
>   For such little chores.

MAK:
>   Good wife, open up quick!   Sees thou not what I bring?

WIFE:
>   I will let thee draw the latch.   Ah, come in my sweeting!

MAK:
>   Yea, thou need not reck'n   on my long standing.

WIFE:
>   By thy naked neck   art thou like to be hung.

MAK:
>   Do away!
>   I am worthy of my meat,   310
>   For in a tight place can I get
>   More than they that swink and sweat,
>   All the long day. *Shows her the sheep.*

Thus it fell to my lot,   Gill; I had such grace.

WIFE:
>   It were a foul blot   to be hanged for that case.

MAK:
>   I have escaped, Gillot,   many such blow in face.

WIFE:
>   "But so long goes the pot   to the water," men says,
>   "At last
>   Comes it home broken".

MAK:

> Well know I that token,   320
> But let it never be spoken.
>> Just come and help, fast!

> I wish it were slain;   I list well to eat!
> This twelvemonth was I not so fain   for a slice of sheep-meat.

WIFE:

> Come they ere it be slain,   and hear the sheep bleat. . . .

MAK:

> Then might I be tane.   That were a cold sweat!
>> Go bar
> The back door.

WIFE:

>> Yes, Mak
> For if they come at thy back. . . .

MAK:

> Then might I get from all the pack,   330
>> The devil's own war.

WIFE:

> A good trick have I spied,   since thou can find none:
> Here shall we him hide,   until they be gone,
> In my cradle. Abide!   Let me alone,
> And I shall lie beside   as in childbed, and groan.

MAK: ·

>> Get set,
> And I shall say thou was light
> Of a knave-child this night.

WIFE:

> Now well is to me the day bright
>> That ever I was bred.   340

> This is good guise,   and a far cast;
> Still a woman's advice   helps at the last.
> I never know who spies: back you go fast.

MAK:

> Unless I come ere they rise,   there will blow a cold blast!
>> I will go sleep.

He returns to the SHEPHERDS.

Still sleeps all this company,
And I shall stalk privily
As it had never been I
> That carried off their sheep.

> *He lies down between them.*

The SHEPHERDS *awake.*

1ST SHEPHERD:
> *Resurrex a mortuus*!   Have hold my hand!   350
> *Judas carnas dominus*!   I can not well stand:
> My foot sleeps, by Jesus.   I totter with hunger — and
> I thought we laid us   full near to England.

2ND SHEPHERD:
> > Ah, yea?
> Lord, how I have slept well!
> As fresh as an eel;
> As light I do feel
> > As leaf on a tree.

3RD SHEPHERD (*Awaking from a nightmare*):
> *Ben'di'té* be herein!   So me quakes,
> My heart is out of my skin,   whatever this makes.   360
> Who makes all this din?   So my brows break!
> To the door will I win.   Hark, fellows, awake!
> > We were four. . . .
> See ye aught of Mak now?

1ST SHEPHERD:
> We were up ere thou.

2ND SHEPHERD:
> Man, I give God a vow,
> > As yet he's gone nowhere.

3RD SHEPHERD:
> Methought he was wrapped   in a wolf-skin.

1ST SHEPHERD:
> So are many wrapped   now, especially within.

3RD SHEPHERD:

> While we had long napped,   methought with a gin   370
> A fat sheep he trapped;   but he made no din.

2ND SHEPHERD:

>   Be still.
> Thy dream maddens thy mood;
> It is but fantasy, by th' rood.

1ST SHEPHERD:

> Now God turn all to good,
>   If it be His will.

2ND SHEPHERD:

> Thou liest too long.   Rise, Mak, for shame!

MAK:

> Now Christ's holy name   be us among!
> What is this? For Saint Jame,   I may not well gang!
> I hope I be the same.   Ah, my neck has laid wrong.   380
>   No more! *They pull him up.*
> Mickle thank! Since yester-even,
> Now by Saint Stephen,
> I was flayed in a dream —
>   My heart was struck sore.

> I thought Gill gan to croak   and labour full sad,
> Well-nigh at first cock,   of a young lad
> For to mend our flock.   Then be I never glad:
> I have more work on my block   than ever I had.
>   Ah, my head!   390
> I've a house-full of young bairns —
> The devil knock out their brains!
> Woe to him that has many bairns,
>   And thereto little bread.

> I must go home, by your leave,   to Gill, as I thought.
> I pray you look to myself,   that I steal nought;
> I am loath you grieve,   or from you take aught.

>   *He goes homewards.*

3RD SHEPHERD:

> Go forth! Ill may you achieve!   Now would I we sought,

This morn,
All our sheep be in store.   400

1ST SHEPHERD:
But I will go before.
Let us meet.

2ND SHEPHERD:
                    Where?

3RD SHEPHERD:
            At the crooked thorn. *Exeunt in different directions.*

MAK *arrives at the door of his cottage; his* WIFE *is within.*

MAK:
Undo this door! Who is here?   How long shall I stand?

WIFE:
Who makes such thunder?   Now go off and be damn'd.

MAK:
Ah, Gill, what cheer?   It is I, Mak, your husband.

WIFE:
Then may we see here   the devil fast-bound.
        Sir Guile!
Lo, he comes with a shriek
As though he were held by the neck.   410
I may not sit at my work
        The shortest while.

MAK (*To audience*):
Will ye hear what fuss she makes   to put up these shows?
She does what she likes,   and plays with her toes.

WIFE:
Why who wanders, who wakes?   Who comes and who goes?
Who brews and who bakes?   What thus makes me hoarse?
        And then
It is ruth to behold:
Now in hot, now in cold,
Full of woes is the household   420
        That wants for a woman.

But what end has thou made   with the herdsmen, Mak?

MAK:

> The last word that they said   when I turned my back:
> They would look that they had   their sheep, all the pack.
> I think they will not be well pleased   when they their sheep lack,
>> Perdy!
> But howso the game goes,
> It is me, they'll suppose;
> And will make a foul noise,
>> And cry out upon me.   430

> But thou must cry out as thou hight.

WIFE:

>>>>> I accord me theretill;
> I shall swaddle him right   in my cradle.
>> *She wraps the sheep up and puts it in the cradle.*
> If it were a greater sleight   yet could I help.
> I will lie down straight.   Come, cover me up.

MAK:

>>>>> I will.

WIFE:

>> Behind!
> Come Coll and his mate,
> They will nip at me tight.

MAK:

> I may cry "Help", outright
>> If the sheep they find.

WIFE:

> Harken for when they call;   they will come at once.   440
> Come, and make ready all,   and sing on thine own;
> Sing "Lullaby" thou shall,   for I must groan,
> And cry out by the wall,   on Mary and John,
>> Full sore.
> Sing out "Lullaby" fast,
> When thou hears them at last.
> If I play not a false cast,
>> Trust me no more.

The SHEPHERDS *enter from different directions.*

3RD SHEPHERD:
    Ah, Coll, good morn!   Why sleepeth thee not?

1ST SHEPHERD:
    Alas, that ever I was born!   We have a foul blot.   450
    A fat wedder have we lorn.

3RD SHEPHERD:
                 Marry, God forbot!

2ND SHEPHERD:
    Who should do us that scorn?   That were a foul spot.

1ST SHEPHERD:
      Some shrew.
    I have sought with my dogs
    All Harbury Moors
    And in fifteen of my young
        Found I but one ewe.

3RD SHEPHERD:
    Now trust me, if ye will;   by Saint Thomas of Kent,
    Either Mak or Gill   to that gave assent.

1ST SHEPHERD:
    Peace man, be still!   I saw when he went.   460
    Thou slanders him ill: thou ought to repent,
        God speed.

2ND SHEPHERD:
    Now as I ever hope to be,
    If I should even here die,
    I would say it were he
        That did that same deed.

3RD SHEPHERD:
    Go we thither, as I reed,   and run on our feet.
    I shall never eat bread,   the sooth till I weet.

1ST SHEPHERD:
    Nor drink in my head,   with him till I meet.

2ND SHEPHERD:
    I will rest in no stead,   till that I him greet,   470
        My brothers.

One promise I hight:
Till I see him in sight,
Shall I never sleep one night
          In same place as others.

They approach MAK's *house: he is singing a lullaby loudly;*
GILL *groans.*

3RD SHEPHERD:
    Will ye hear how they hack?   Our sire likes to croon!

1ST SHEPHERD:
    Heard I never one crake   so clear out of tune.
    Call on him.

2ND SHEPHERD:
                    Mak,   undo your door soon!

MAK:
    Who is that spake,   as if it were noon,
              Aloft?   480
    Who is that I say?

3RD SHEPHERD:
    Good fellows, were it day.

MAK:
    As far as ye may, *He opens the door.*
              Good sirs, speak soft,

    Over a sick woman's head,   that is ill at ease.
    I had liefer be dead   than she had any disease.

WIFE:
    Go to another stead!   I may not well wheeze,
    Each footstep ye tread   goes through my nose
              So loudly.

1ST SHEPHERD:
    Tell us Mak, if ye may,   490
    How fare ye, I say?

MAK:
    What are ye in town today?
              Now, how fare thee?

Ye have run in the mire,   and are wet yet;
I shall make you a fire,   if ye will sit.
A nurse would I hire.   Remember it yet?
Well quit is my hire —   my dream: this is it —
      For a season.
I have bairns, if ye knew
Well more than enough;   500
But we must drink as we brew,
      And that is but reason.

I would ye had dined ere ye go.   Methinks that ye sweat.

2ND SHEPHERD:
    Nay, neither mendeth our mood   — neither drink nor meat.

MAK:
    Why, sir, ails ye ought but good?

3RD SHEPHERD:
                    Yea, our sheep that we get
    Are stolen as they go.   Our loss is great.

MAK:
      Sirs, drink!
    Had I been there
    Some had bought it sore.

1ST SHEPHERD:
    Marry, some men trow that ye were,   510
      And that us forthink.

2ND SHEPHERD:
    Mak, some men suppose   that it should be thee.

3RD SHEPHERD:
    Either thee or thy spouse,   so say we.

MAK:
    Now if ye have suppose   to Gill or to me,
    Come rip open our house,   and then may ye see
      Who had her.
      The SHEPHERDS *begin to search the house.*
    If I any sheep got,
    Either cow or stot —
    And Gill, my wife rose not
      Here since she laid her —   520

As I am true and loyal,   to God here I pray
That this be the first meal   that I shall eat this day.

>   *He points to the cradle.*

1ST SHEPHERD:

Mak, as I hope to be well,   advise thee, I say:
He learned timely to steal   that could not say nay.

WIFE:

I swelt!
Out, thieves, from my home!
Ye come to rob us to the bone.

MAK:

Hear ye not how she groan?
Your hearts should melt!

The SHEPHERDS *approach the cradle.*

WIFE:

Away, thieves, from my nursling.   Come near him not there! 530

MAK:

Wist ye how she was labouring,   your hearts would be sore.
Ye do wrong, I give warning,   that thus come in before
A woman has been farrowing —   but I say no more.

WIFE:

Ooh! My middle!
I pray God so mild,
If ever I ye beguild,
That I *eat* this child
That lies in this cradle.

MAK:

Peace, woman, for God's pain,   and cry not so!
Thou spills all thy brain,   and makes me full woe.   540

2ND SHEPHERD:

I trow our sheep be slain.   What find ye two?

3RD SHEPHERD:

All work we in vain: we may as well go.
Only tatters!
I can find no flesh,
Hard or nesh,

Salt or fresh —
>Only two empty platters.

(Pointing to the cradle)
Living beast besides this,   tame or wild,
None, so have I bliss —   as strong as it smelled.

WIFE:
>No! God gi'me bliss,   and give me joy of my child!   550

1ST SHEPHERD:
>We have marked amiss.   I hold us beguild.

2ND SHEPHERD (*To* MAK):
>>Sir, we've done.
>But Sir — our Lady him save! —
>Is your child girl or knave?

MAK:
>Any lord might him have
>>This child to his son.

When awake he can grip: joy is it to see!

3RD SHEPHERD:
>May his life have good hap   and long be lucky.
>But who acted as gossip   and so soon were ready?

MAK:
>Ah! Fair fall each lip.

1ST SHEPHERD (*Aside*):
>>Hark now, a lie.   560

MAK:
>>So, God them thank,
>Perkin and Gibon Waller, I say,
>And gentle John Horn, in good fay —
>He made all th' affray —
>>He with the long shank.

2ND SHEPHERD:
>Mak, friends will we be,   for we are all one.

MAK:
>We? Now I hold back, me,   for amends get I none.
>Fare well all three!   (*Aside*) All glad were ye gone.

3RD SHEPHERD:

>Fair words may there be,   but love is there none
>>This year. *The* SHEPHERDS *leave the house.*   570

1ST SHEPHERD:

>Gave ye the child anything?

2ND SHEPHERD:

>I trow not one farthing.

3RD SHEPHERD:

>Fast again will I fling:
>>Abide ye me there. *He runs back.*

>Mak, take it to no grief   if I come to thy bairn.

MAK:

>Nay, thou does me great reproof,   and foul thyself borne.

3RD SHEPHERD:

>The child will not grieve,   that little day-starne.
>Mak, with your leave,   let me give your bairn
>>But six pence.

MAK:

>Nay, have done. He sleeps.   580

3RD SHEPHERD:

>Methinks that he peeps.

MAK:

>When he wakens he weeps.
>>I pray you go hence!

>*The other* SHEPHERDS *return.*

3RD SHEPHERD:

>Give me leave him to kiss,   and lift up the clout.
>What the devil is this?   He has a long snout!

1ST SHEPHERD:

>He is marked amiss.   We should not pry about.

2ND SHEPHERD:

>Ill-spun weft, iwis,   ever comes badly out.
>>Aye, so!
>He is like to our sheep.

3RD SHEPHERD:

    Ho, Gib, may I peep?   590

1ST SHEPHERD:

    I trow nature will creep

        Where it may not go.

2ND SHEPHERD:

    This was a quaint gaud,   and a far cast;

    It was a fine fraud.

3RD SHEPHERD:

               Yea, sirs, was't.

    Let us burn this bawd   and bind her fast.

    A false scold   does hang at the last;

        So shall thou.

    Will ye see how they swaddle

    His four feet in the middle?

    Saw I never in a cradle   600

        A horned lad ere now.

MAK:

    Peace, bid I. What,   let be your uproar!

    I am he that him gat,   and yond woman him bare.

1ST SHEPHERD:

    What name shall be he hat?   Mak? By God, he's Mak's heir!

2ND SHEPHERD:

    Let be all that!   Now God send him care!

        I saw.

WIFE:

    As pretty child is he,

    As sits on woman's knee;

    A dillydon, perdy,

        To cause a man laugh.   610

3RD SHEPHERD:

    I know him by the ear-mark: that is a sure token.

MAK:

    I tell you, sirs — hark! —   his nose was broken.

    And then told me a clerk   that witchcraft had spoken.

1ST SHEPHERD:
>   This was a false work;   revenge must be wreaken.
>   Get weapon!

WIFE:
>   He was taken by an elf;
>   I saw it myself.
>   When the clock struck twelve
>   Was he forshapen.

2ND SHEPHERD:
>   Ye two are both deft,   and belong in one stead.   620

1ST SHEPHERD:
>   Since they hold to their theft,   let us do them to death.

MAK:
>   If I trespass hereaft',   strike off my head.
>   With you the matter be left.

3RD SHEPHERD:
>   Sirs, do my reed:
>   For this trespass
>   We will neither ban nor flite,
>   Fight nor chide,
>   But have done forthright
>   And toss him in a canvass.

They toss MAK *in a tarpaulin or blanket, and return to the fields.*

1ST SHEPHERD:
>   Lord, how I am sore,   at point for to burst!
>   In faith, I can no more;   therefore will I rest.   630

2ND SHEPHERD:
>   As a sheep of seven score   he weighed in my fist.
>   For to sleep anywhere   methink that I list.

3RD SHEPHERD:
>   Now I pray you
>   Lie down on this ground.

1ST SHEPHERD:
>   These thieves stay still in my mind.

3RD SHEPHERD:
>Wherefore should ye be pained?
>>Do as I say you. *They lie down to sleep.*

There is a bright light and the ANGEL *appears above.*

ANGEL (*Sings*):
>*Gloria in excelsis.*

>(*To* SHEPHERDS)
>Rise herdsmen kind,   for now is He born
>That shall take from the fiend   what Adam did lorn;
>That warlock to confound,   this night is He born.   640
>God is made your friend,   now on this morn,
>>He behests.
>At Beth'lem go see;
>There lies that Lord free,
>In a crib full poorly,
>>Betwixt two beasts. *Exit. A star remains.*

1ST SHEPHERD:
>This was as quaint steyven   as ever yet I heard.
>It is a marvel to namen,   thus to be scared.

2ND SHEPHERD:
>Of God's Son in heaven   he spake unaffeared.
>The trees did blaze and lighten: methought he so made   650
>>Them appear.

3RD SHEPHERD:
>He spake of a bairn
>In Beth'lem, I you warn.

1ST SHEPHERD:
>That betokens yond starne:
>>Let us seek Him there.

2ND SHEPHERD:
>Say, what was his song?   Heard ye not how he crak'd it,
>Three breves to one long?

3RD SHEPHERD:
>>Yea marry, he hacked it:
>No crotchet was wrong,   nor nothing lacked it.

1ST SHEPHERD:
> Now to sing us among,   right as he knocked it,
>> I can.   660

2ND SHEPHERD:
> Let us see how ye croon.
> Can ye bark at the moon?

3RD SHEPHERD:
> Hold your tongues! Have done!

1ST SHEPHERD:
>> Hark after me then. *He sings, and the others join in.*

2ND SHEPHERD:
> To Beth'lem he bad   that we should gang:
> I am full afraid   that we tarry too long.

3RD SHEPHERD:
> Be merry and not sad: of mirth is our song!
> Everlastingly glad,   for reward may we gain,
>> Without any let.

1ST SHEPHERD:
> Hie we thither surely,   670
> Though we be wet and weary,
> To that Child and that Lady;
>> We must not it forget. *He begins to sing again.*

2ND SHEPHERD:
> We find by the prophecy —   Let be your din! —
> Of David and Isay   and more than I mind —
> They prophesied learnedly —   that in a virgin
> Should he alight and lie,   to overset our sin,
>> And slake it —
> Our kind — from woe.
> For Isay said so: 680
> *Ecce virgo*
>> *Concipiet* a child that is naked.

3RD SHEPHERD:
> Full glad may we be,   and abide the day
> That lovely Child to see,   who all mighty deeds may.

Lord, well were me,   for once and for aye,
Might I kneel on my knee,   some word for to say
      To that Child.
But the angel said
In a crib was He laid;
He was poorly arrayed,   690
      Both meanly and mild.

1ST SHEPHERD:
Patriarchs that have been,   and prophets beforn,
All desired to have seen   this Child that is born.
They are gone away clean: that sight have they lorn.
But we shall see Him, I ween,   ere it be morn,
      By this token.
When I see Him and feel,
Then wot I full well
It is true as steel
      That the prophets have spoken: 700

To so poor as we are   He would appear —
Find us first, and declare   by His messenger.

2ND SHEPHERD:
Go we now; let us fare.   The place is us near.

3RD SHEPHERD:
I am ready and yare,   go we together
      To that Bright.
Lord if thy will it be —
We are lewd all three —
Thou grant us something of glee
      To comfort Thy mite. *They enter the stable.*

1ST SHEPHERD:
Hail, comely and clean!   Hail, young Child!   710
Hail, Maker, as I mean,   of a maiden so mild!
Thou has confounded, I ween,   the warlock so wild:
The false bringer of teen,   now goes beguiled.
      Lo merry He is!
Lo, He laughs, my Sweeting!
Ah, a very fair meeting!
I have held to my telling:
      Have a bob of cherries.

2ND SHEPHERD:

>Hail, Sovreign Saviour,   for Thou hast us sought!
>Hail, Nurseling and Flower,   that all things has wrought!   720
>Hail, Full of Favour,   that made all out of nought!
>Hail! I kneel and I cower.   A bird have I brought
>>To my Bairn.
>Hail, little tiny Mop!
>Of our creed Thou art crop.
>I would drink of Thy cup,
>>Little Day-starne.

3RD SHEPHERD:

>Hail, little darling Dear,   full of Godhead!
>I pray Thee be near   when that I have need.
>Hail, Sweet in Thy cheer!   My heart will bleed   730
>To see Thee sit here   in so poor a weed,
>>With no pennies.
>Hail! Put forth Thy dall.
>I bring Thee but a ball:
>Have and play Thee withall,
>>And go to the tennis.

MARY:

>The Father of heaven,   God omnipotent,
>That set all in days seven,   His Son has He sent.
>My name did He namen,   and on me His light spent!
>I conceived Him full even   by God's might as He meant;   740
>>And now is He born.
>May He keep you from woe!
>I shall pray Him so.
>Tell forth as ye go,
>>And mind on this morn.

1ST SHEPHERD:

>Farewell Lady,   so fair to behold,
>With thy Child on thy knee.

2ND SHEPHERD:

>>>But He lies full cold.
>Lord, it is well for me!   Now we go, Thou behold.

3RD SHEPHERD:
> Forsooth, already   this story seems to be told
> > Full oft.   750

1ST SHEPHERD:
> What grace we have found!

2ND SHEPHERD:
> Come, for us, all is won!

3RD SHEPHERD:
> To sing are we bound —
> > Let's take it aloft. *Exeunt, singing.*

Characters

MESSENGER
HEROD
1ST KNIGHT
2ND KNIGHT
3RD KNIGHT
1ST COUNSELLOR
2ND COUNSELLOR
1ST WOMAN and her CHILD
2ND WOMAN and her CHILD
3RD WOMAN and her CHILD

The KNIGHTS can be provided with armourers and attendants, and the number of KNIGHTS and WOMEN can be increased. HEROD can be provided with attendants.

The CHILDREN are dolls.

Staging

A throne for HEROD must dominate the acting area. At some distance, there is a place for the KNIGHTS and their armourers, and a place for the WOMEN and their CHILDREN.

V Herod the Great

Trumpets. Enter Herod's MESSENGER, *and addresses the
audience.*

MESSENGER:

    Most mighty Mahown'   mingle joy and mirth!
    To men of borough and town,   from fell and from firth,
    To both King with crown   and Barons by birth,
    To all who will keep voices down,   a peace of great worth
            Shall behap.
    Take careful attent
    What greetings are sent,
    Else harms shall ye hent
            And troubles shall you wrap.

Reads from a proclamation

Herod, the High King   — by grace of Mahown' —   10
Of Jewry, surmounting   sternly with crown
All on earth that are living   in tower and in town,
Graciously you greeting,   commands you be bound
            At his bidding.
Love him with loyalty!
Dread him who is doughty!
He charges you be ready,
            Lowly, and to his liking.

What man upon mould   against him shall complain
His teen shall be told,   whether knight, squire or swain.   20
Be he never so bold,   buys he that bargain
Twelve thousand fold   more than I sayn,
            Ye may trust.
He is wonderly worthy,
Uncouthly sorry:

For a boy that is born hereby
      Stands he distressed.

A king they him call,   and that we deny.
How should it so fall,   great marvel have I:
Therefore over all   shall I make a cry   30
That ye try not to bawl,   nor like not to lie
      At this tide.
Carp of no King
But Herod, that lording,
Or dart to your dwelling
      Your heads for to hide.

He is King of kings   in his kind, I know,
Chief Lord of lordings,   chief Leader of law.
There wait under his wings   those that bold boasts will blow;
Great dukes down ding   'fore him in great awe   40
      And bow down.
Tuscany and Turkey,
All India and Italy,
Syria and Sicily
      Dread his renown.

From Paradise to Padua,   to Montefiascon
From Egypt to Mantua   unto Yorktown,
From Sarceny to Susa,   to Greece and all round,
Both Normandy and Norway,   bow down to his crown.
      His renown   50
Can no tongue tell,
From heaven unto hell;
Of him can none spell
      But his cousin, Mahown'.

He is the worthiest of all   bairns that are born;
Free men are his thrall,   full teenfully torn.
Begin he to brawl,   many men catch his scorn!
Obey must we all,   or else ye be lorn
      At once.
Drop down on your knee,   60
All that him do see:
Displeased he be
      And breaks many bones.

Here he cometh now, I cry: that lord I foretold!
Fast afore will I hie,   running full bold
And welcoming him worshipfully,   laughing threefold,
As he is most worthy,   and kneel on the mould
      So low;
Down dutifully fall
Before rank most royal;   70
Hail, the worthiest of all
      To thee must I bow.

Music: enter HEROD, *accompanied by* KNIGHTS *and*
COUNSELLORS. *The* MESSENGER *kneels.*

Hail, beloved Lord! Lo!   Thy letters have I relayed:
I have done what I could do,   and for peace I have prayed;
And much more thereunto   openly displayed.
But rumour is rife so   that boldly they brayed
      Amongst them.
They carp of a king;
They cease not such chattering

HEROD:
      But I shall tame their talking   80
            And let them go hang them.

Stint, scoundrels, your din!   — Yea, everyone!
I reed that ye harken   until I be gone;
For if I begin,   I break every bone,
And pull from the skin   the carcass anon —
      Yea, perdy!
Cease all this wonder,
And make us no blunder,
For I'll rive you in sunder
      Be ye so hardy.   90

Peace, both young and old —   at my bidding, I said —
For by me all is controll'd: through me are you living or dead.
Whoever that is bold,   I bash him in the head!
Speak not ere I have told   what I will in this stead.
      Ye wot not
All that I must receive.
Stir ye not without leave;

For if ye do, I'll cleave
    You small, as flesh for the pot.

My mirths are turned to teen,   my meekness into ire,   100
And all for one, I ween,   I feel within me fire.
If I see him with eyen,   I shall give him his hire:
Unless I do as I mean,   I were a full lewd sire
    Beyond any one.
Had I that lad in hand,
As I am king in land,
I should with this steel brand
    Break his every bone.

My name springs far and near: the doughtiest, men me call,
That ever ran with spear,   a lord and king royal.   110
What joy have I to hear   of a lad to seize my stall!
If I this crown may wear,   that boy shall pay for all:
    My anger!
I wot not what the devil me ails;
They tease me so with tales
That, by our dear God's nails,
    I will be quiet no longer.

Ah devil! methink I burst   for anger and for teen;
I trow these kings be passed   that here with me have been.
They promised me full fast   ere now here to be seen,   120
Or else I should have cast   another sleight, I ween.
    I tell you,
A boy they said they sought,
With offering that they brought;
It moves my heart right nought
    To break his neck in two.

But be they passed me by,   by Mahown' in heaven,
I shall — to this I hie —   set all at odds and even.
Trow ye a king as I   will suffer them to namen
Any to have mastery   but myself full even?   130
    As I have life,
The devil me hang and draw,
Once that young lout I know,
If I give him not a blow
    That of life shall him deprive.

For fear of worse, I would   be glad if the kings were gone.
If ye thereof hear told: I pray you say anon.
For if they be so bold,   by God that sits on throne,
The pain cannot be told   that they shall have each one,
      For ire.   140
Of such pains never man heard tell,
So ugly and so fell,
When Lucifer in hell
      Their bones shall tear and fire.

1ST KNIGHT:

      Lord, think not ill if I   tell you how they are passed;
      I keep nothing concealed, truly.   Since they came to you last
      Another way, more speedily,   they sought, and that full fast.

HEROD:

      Why, and have they passed me by?   Wei! Out! for teen I burst!
         Wei! Fy!

He strides round the stage, beating the KNIGHTS.

      Fie on the devil! Where can I bide,   150
      Unless I fight and terribly chide?
      Thieves, I say! Ye should have spied
         And told when they went by.

      Are ye knights to trust?   Nay, louts ye are, and thieves!
      I'll sure yield up my ghost,   so sore my heart it grieves.

2ND KNIGHT:

      What need you be aghast?   There are no great mischiefs
      To make your teeth to gnash.

3RD KNIGHT:

                          Why make ye such reproofs
         Withouten cause?
      Thus should ye not treat us,
      And ungainly so beat us;   160
      Ye should not rebuke us
         Withouten wiser words.

HEROD:

      Fie, loggerheads and liars!   Lazy louts, each one!
      Traitors and far worse!   Knaves, and knights none!

Had ye been worth your ears,   thus had they not gone.
Get I those land-beggars,   I'll break their every bone.
                First vengeance
Shall I see on their bones.
(*To the absent kings*)
If ye stay here on your owns,
I shall ding you with stones —   170
                Yes, *sans doutance*!

I wot not where I may sit   for anger and for teen.
We have not done all yet,   if all be as I ween.
Fie! devil! Now how is it?   As long as I have eyen,
I think not for to flit,   but King I will be seen
                For ever.
If I stay in good heart,
I tell you what is my part:
I will cause them to start
                Or else trust me never.   180

1ST KNIGHT:

Sir, they went suddenly   ere any man wist,
Else we had met — yea, perdy! —   and that may ye trust.

2ND KNIGHT:

So bold nor so hardy   against our list
Was none of that company;   none durst meet me with fist
                Being afeard.

3RD KNIGHT:

They darest not abide
But ran them to hide;
Might I one of them spied
                I had plucked at his beard.

What could we more do   to save your honour?   190

2ND KNIGHT:

We were ready thereto   and shall be any hour.

HEROD:

Now, since it is so,   ye shall have favour.
Go where'ere you will go,   by town and by tower.

        Go forth! *Exeunt* KNIGHTS.
I have matters to mull
With my Privy Council.
(*To* COUNSELLORS)
Clerks, ye hear the bell;
        Ye must give your report.

One spake in mine ear   a wonderful saying,
And said a maiden should bear   some other to be king.   200
Sirs, I pray you enquire   in all writing,
In Virgil, in Homer,   and all other thing,
        Saving hearsay.
Seek stories in verse,
But leave Epistles and worse,
Like Mattins and Mass,
        All these I gainsay.

The COUNSELLORS *search through many books.*

I pray you tell me kindly   now, what ye find.

1ST COUNSELLOR:
    Truly, sir, prophecy   is not blind.
    We read thus in Isay: "He shall be so kind,   210
    That a maiden, truly,   who has never sinned,
        Shall him bear."
    "*Virgo concipiet*
    Natumque pariet":
    "Emanuel" is fit
        For the name he does bear.

    "God is with us",   that is for to say.

2ND COUNSELLOR:
    And others say thus,   trust me ye may:
    "At Beth'lem a gracious   lord shall have his way,
    That of Jewry mighteous   king shall be for aye,   220
        Lord mighty;
    And him shall honour
    Both king and emperor."

HEROD:
    Why! Should I to him cower?
        Nay, there thou lies lightly.

Fie! The devil thee speed —   and me, before I drink once! —
This has thou done indeed   to anger me for the nonce;
And thou, knave, thou thy mede   shall have, by God's
                                              dear bones!
Thou knowest not half thy creed.   Out, thieves, from my
                                              homes!
         Fie knaves!   230
Fie, dotty-polls, with your books —
Go, cast them, in the brooks!
With such wiles and crooks,
      My wit flies and raves.

Heard I never such a trick,   that a knave so slight
Should come like the meek   and reave me out of my right.
Nay, his body shall creak: I shall cut him down straight!
Ware! I say, I will him seek.   Now think I to fight
      For anger.
My guts will out-thring   240
Unless this lad is hung;
Unless I have revenging,
      I may live no longer.

Should a child in a cave,   but of one year of age,
Thus make me to rave?

1ST COUNSELLOR:

                Sir, quieten this outrage!
Away let ye wave   all such language,
Your honour to save.   Is he aught but a page
      Of one year?
We two shall be his bane,
Between our wits so keen;   250
If ye do just as I mean,
      He shall die on a spear.

2ND COUNSELLOR:

For fear that he reign,   do as we reed:
Throughout Bethelem   and every other stead,
Give knights instruction   to put unto dead
All knave-children   of two years bred
      And less.

This child's life may ye spill
Thus at your own will.

HEROD:

> Now, as thou says theretill,   260
> > This is right noble jest.

> If I live in my land   a good life as I hope,
> This dare I thee warrant —   to make thee a Pope!
> O, my heart's buoyant —   and now in a gallop!
> For this noblest of plan,   thou shall have a drop
> > Of my good grace:
> Marks, rentals and pounds,
> Great castles and their grounds;
> Through all seas and sounds,
> > I give thee rights of the chase.   270

> Now will I proceed   and take vengeance.
> (*To the* MESSENGER)
> All the flower of knighthood   call to allegiance,
> *Beau sire*, I thee bid: it may thee advance.

MESSENGER:

> Lord, I shall me speed   and bring, perchance,
> > To thy sight.

He leaves HEROD *and calls out.*

> Hark, knights, I you bring
> Here the new tiding:
> Unto Herod, the king,
> > Haste you with all might.

Trumpet music.

> In all the haste ye may,   in armour full bright;   280
> In your best of array   look that ye be dight!

1ST KNIGHT:

> Why should we make fray?

2ND KNIGHT:

> > > This is not all right.

3RD KNIGHT:

> Sirs, withouten delay,   I fear that we shall fight.

MESSENGER:

> I pray you
> As fast as ye may
> Come to him this day.

1ST KNIGHT:

> What, in our best array?

MESSENGER:

> Yea, sirs, I say unto you.

Music. The KNIGHTS *start to get into their armour.*

2ND KNIGHT:

> Somewhat is in hand,   whatever it may mean.

3RD KNIGHT:

> Tarry not just to stand   around, ere we have been.   290

They go to HEROD *in haste.*

MESSENGER:

> King Herod, all regnant,   well be ye seen!
> Your knights are at command   with armour in full sheen,
> > At your will.

1ST KNIGHT:

> Hail, doughtiest of all!
> We are come at your call
> For to do what we shall
> > Your lust to fulfil.

HEROD:

> Welcome lordings, iwis,   both great and small!
> The cause now is this   that I send for you all:
> A lad, a knave, born is   that should be king royal;   300
> Unless I kill both him and his,   I wot I burst my gall.
> > Therefore, sirs,
> Vengeance shall ye take,
> All for that lad's sake;
> And Great Men I shall you make,
> > Where ye come anywhere, sirs.

> To Beth'lem look ye go,   and all the coast about;
> All knave children must you   slay — look that ye be stout —

Of years if they be two   and less. Of all that rout,
Alive leave none of those   that lie in swaddling clout,   310
        I reed you.
Spare you no kin's blood,
Let all run in a flood.
If women do wax wode,
        I warn you, sirs to speed you.

Hence now go your way,   so you will be soon there!

2ND KNIGHT:
    I wot we make a fray,   but I will go on before.

3RD KNIGHT:
    Ah! think sirs, I say;   I must whet my tusk, like boar.

1ST KNIGHT:
    Set me in front, aye!   I'm good to catch a score!
    (*To* HEROD)
        Hail, gently!   320
    We shall for your sake
    Some doleful sport make.

HEROD:
    If well my wrong you wreak,
        Ye shall find me friendly.

    The KNIGHTS *leave to military music.*

2ND KNIGHT:
    Go follow now our note,   and do all for our weal.

3RD KNIGHT:
    I shall beat them on their coat;   begin I now to revel!

    The 1ST WOMAN *meets them with her* CHILD.

1ST KNIGHT:
    Hark, fellows, now ye dote!   Yonder comes the miserable.
    I wager here a groat,   she will not like me well
        Before we part.
    (*To* 1ST WOMAN)
    Dame, think it not ill   330
    Thy knave if I kill.   *He makes a grab for it.*

1ST WOMAN:
> What, Thief! Against my will?
>> Lord, keep him in good heart! *She tries to escape.*

1ST KNIGHT:
> Bide still now; abide.   No further thou goes.

1ST WOMAN:
> Be quiet, thief! Shall I chide   and make here a noise?

1ST KNIGHT:
> I shall rob thee of thy pride.   Kill we now these boys!

1ST WOMAN:
> Come what may betide,   keep down thy nose,
>> False thief!
> Here's a blow for thy head!

1ST KNIGHT:
> What, whore, are thou wode?   *He kills her* CHILD.   340

1ST WOMAN:
> Out, alas, my child's blood
>> Shame on thee, without reprieve!

> Alas for shame and sin!   Alas that I was born!
> Of weeping who may stint,   to see her child forlorn?
> My comfort and my kin,   my son, thus all is torn!
> Vengeance for this sin   I cry, both eve and morn.

2ND KNIGHT:
>> Well done!
> Come, thou old bag, nigh!   *He grabs* 2ND WOMAN.
> That lad of thine shall die.

2ND WOMAN:
> Mercy, Lord, I cry!   350
>> It is mine own dear son.

2ND KNIGHT:
> No mercy shall thou receive;   it does nothing for thee, Maud.

2ND WOMAN:
> Then thy scalp shall I cleave!   List thou to be clawed?
> Leave off, leave, leave!

2ND KNIGHT:
> Peace, I bid thee, bawd!

2ND WOMAN:
> Fie, fie, for reprieve!   Fie, you're full of fraud —
>> No man!
> Have at thy tabard,
> Whoremaster and bastard!
> Thou shall not be spared!
>> I cry and I ban!   *He kills her* CHILD.   360

> Out! Murder, I say,   traitor strong and thief!
> Out, alas, and wey-allay,   my child that was so lief!
> My love, my blood, my play,   that never did man grief!
> Alas, alas, this day!   I would my heart should cleave
>> In sunder!
> Vengeance I cry and call
> On Herod and his knights all.
> Vengeance, Lord, upon them fall,
>> And mickle world's wonder!

3RD KNIGHT:
> This is as well-wrought gear   as ever that may be.   370
> (*To* 3RD WOMAN)
> Come hitherward, here!   Ye need not to fly.

3RD WOMAN:
> Will you do any drear,   unto my child and me?

3RD KNIGHT:
> He shall die, I thee swear: His heart-blood shall thou see.

3RD WOMAN:
>> God forbid. *He kills her* CHILD.
> Thief, thou shed'st my child's blood!
> Out, I cry! I go near wode!
> Alas, my heart is all in flood,
>> To see my child thus bleed.

> By God, thou shall never buy   penance for what th'hast done.

3RD KNIGHT:
> That I shall never try,   by sun or by moon.   380

3RD WOMAN:

Have at thee, say I!   Take that for a foin!

She attacks him.

Out on thee, I cry!   Have at thy groin,
>
> Another!

This one keep I in store.

3RD KNIGHT:

Peace now, no more!

3RD WOMAN:

I cry and I roar,
>
> Out on thee, man-murderer!

Alas, my babe, my innocent,   child of my flesh! For sorrow
That God has dearly sent,   what pain may I ever borrow?
Thy body to pieces is all rent!   I cry, both eve and morrow, 390
Vengeance for thy blood thus spent: "Fie!" I cry, and
>
> "Harrow!"

1ST KNIGHT:

> Go quickly!

Get up from these stones,
Ye old trots. Go all at once;
Or by God's own dear bones
> I'll make you go more quickly!

Exeunt WOMEN, *with their dead* CHILDREN.

They are frightened now, I wot;   they will not abide.

2ND KNIGHT:

Let us run foot-hot   — now would I we hurried —
And tell of this lot,   how we have betide.

3RD KNIGHT:

Thou can follow thy note: that have I espied.   400
> Go forth now,

Tell thou Herod our tale.
For all our avail,
I tell you, *sans* fail,
> He will us credit allow.

1ST KNIGHT:

I am best of you all,   and ever has been;

The devil have my soul   but I be the first seen!
It's fitting for me to first call   on my lord, as I ween.

2ND KNIGHT:

What needs thee to brawl?   Be not so keen
          In this anger.   410
I shall say thou did best —
'Cept myself, as I guessed.

1ST KNIGHT:

Wei! This is most honest.

3RD KNIGHT:

          Go, tarry no longer. *They go to* HEROD.

Trumpets sound.

1ST KNIGHT:

Hail, Herod, our king!   Full glad may ye be;
Good tidings we bring.   Harken now unto me.
We have made riding   throughout all Jewry.
Well wit ye one thing: that murdered have we
          Many thousands.

2ND KNIGHT:

I made them full hot: 420
I paid them in their cot.
Their dams, I may wot,
          Will ne'er bind them in bands.

3RD KNIGHT:

Had ye seen how I fared   when I came among them!
There was none that I spared,   but laid on and dang them.
I am worthy a reward.   When I was among them,
I stood and I stared: no pity to hang them
          Had I.

HEROD:

Now by mighty Mahown',
That is good of renown,   430
If I bear this crown
          Ye shall have a lady

Each one to him laid,   and to wed at his will.

1ST KNIGHT (*Aside*):

So have ye long said — do somewhat theretil!

2ND KNIGHT:

And I was never afraid, for good nor for ill.

3RD KNIGHT:

Ye might hold you well paid   our desire to fulfil,
        Thus think me,
With treasure untold:
If it pleased that ye would,
Both silver and gold   440
        To give us great plenty.

HEROD:

As I am king crowned,   I think it quite right;
There goes none on ground   that has such a wight.
A hundred thousand pound   is good wage for a knight;
Of pennies good and round,   now may you go light
        With great store.
And ye knights of ours
Should have castles and towers,
Both to you and to yours,
        For now and evermore.   450

1ST KNIGHT:

Was never none born,   by downs nor by dales,
Nor none us beforn,   that had such avails,

2ND KNIGHT:

We have castles and corn,   and much gold in our mails.

3RD KNIGHT:

It will ne'er be out-worn,   whatever our tales.
        Hail, gently!
Hail Lord! Hail King!
We are forth hastening.

HEROD:

May Mahown' now you bring
        Where he is lord friendly!   *Exeunt* KNIGHTS.

Now in peace may I stand —   I thank thee Mahown'! —   460
And give of my land   that longs to my crown.

(*To audience*)
Come therefore merchant,   both of burgh and of town,
Pounds, each one, a thousand,   when I am in town,
     Shall ye have.
I shall be full fain
To give that I sayn;
Wait till I come again
     And then ye may crave.

It seems to be good,   now my heart is at ease,
That I shed so much blood.   At peace, all my riches!   470
For to see this flood   from the feet to the noses
Moves nothing my mood   — I laugh so hard that I wheeze!
     Ah Mahown',
So light is my soul
That all of sugar is my gall!
I may do what I shall
     And bear up my crown.

I was cast down in care,   so frightfully afraid;
But I need not despair,   for low is he laid
That I most dread e'er;   I have him so flayed.   480
Or else it wonder were —   when so many strayed
     Insecure —
That one should be hurtless
And 'scape away helpless,
Where so many babies
     Their harms may not recure.

A hundred thousand, I wot,   and forty are slain,
And four thousand. Thereat   I ought to be fain.
Such a murder on a flat   shall never be again.
Had I had but one smack   at that villain   490
     So young,
It should have been spoken
How I had me wreaken,
When I'm dead and rotten,
     With many a tongue.

Thus shall I teach knave,   example to take,
He whose wits do rave   such mastery to make:

Wantonness should you waive;   let your talk not crake:
No sovereign shall you save.   Your neck shall I shake
      In sunder.   500
On no King let ye call
But on Herod, the royal,
Or else many one shall
      Upon your bodies wonder.

If I hear anything spoke   when I come again,
Your brains will be broke;   therefore be sure to obey.
All meaning will I unlock: it shall be so plain.
If I begin with rage to rock,   I'll think all disdain
      Over fancified!
Sirs, this is my counsel   510
Be not too cruel
But *adieu*. . . . to the devil!
      I can speak no more Frenchified. *Exit.*

Characters
1ST TORTURER
2ND TORTURER
JESUS
CAIAPHAS
ANNAS
FROWARD, the Torturers' servant.

Staging
Two raised thrones are placed side by side, centre-stage.

VI The Buffetting

Enter 1ST *and* 2ND TORTURERS *driving* JESUS *(with bound hands) before them as if He were an animal: He has already been arraigned before Pilate for the first time.*

1ST TORTURER:

    Go on, gee up, go!   And trot on apace.

    To Annas will we go,   and Sir Caiaphas.

    Wit thou well of them two   get'st thou no grace

    But everlasting woe,   for thou has trespassed

        So mickle.

    Thy miss is more

    Than ever gets thou grace for!

    Thou has been, everywhere and more,

        Full false and full fickle.

2ND TORTURER:

    It is a wonder to see,   thus to be ganging: 10

    We have had for thee   mickle heart-searching,

    But at last shall we be   out of heart-longing,

    When thou has heard two or three   sayings, each worth a

                     hanging.

       No wonder!

    Such wiles can thou make,

    Get the people to forsake

    Our laws, and thine take:

        Thus is it that thou blunder.

1ST TORTURER:

    Thou cannot speak against't,   if thou be true.

    Some men hold thee a saint,   and that shall thou rue.   20

    Fair words can thou paint   and lay down laws new.

2ND TORTURER:

    Now be ye attaint,   for we will pursue

This matter.
Many words has thou said
With which are we not pleased.
As good that thou had
        Holden still thy chatter.

1ST TORTURER:

It is better sit still   than rise up and fall:
Thou has long had thy will,   and made many a brawl;
At the last would thou kill   and fordo us all   30
Though we never did ill.

2ND TORTURER:
                    I am sure he shall
        Not endure it;
For if other men praise him,
We shall accuse him.
Himself shall not excuse him,
        To you I ensure it,

With no legal parlance.

1ST TORTURER:
                Fain would he wink,
Or falsify countenance —   I say as I think.

2ND TORTURER:
He has done us grievance,   therefore bitter shall he drink.
He shall have great mischance   that has made us swink   40
        In walking,
So that hardly may I more.

1ST TORTURER:
Peace, man, we are there!
I shall walk in before
        And tell of his talking.

They approach CAIAPHAS *and* ANNAS *on the Judgement
Seats.*

Hail, sirs, as ye sit,   so worthy among men!
Why asked ye not yet   how we've fared with this one?

2ND TORTURER:
Sir, we would fain ye wit   all weary are our bones!

We have had discomfit   right ill for this once —
      He so tarried   50

CAIAPHAS:
    Say, were ye ought adread?
    Were ye ought wrong led,
    Or in dangerous stead?
        Sirs, who has miscarried?

ANNAS:
    Say, were ye ought in doubt   for fault of light,
    As ye watched roundabout?

1ST TORTURER:
                Sir, as I am true knight,
    Of my mother since I sucked   had I never such a night.
    Mine eyes have not locked   together right
        Since morrow.
    But yet I think it well set   60
    Since we with this traitor met. *He points to* JESUS.
    Sir, this is he that forfeit,
        And has done so much sorrow.

CAIAPHAS:
    Can ye ought him appeach?   Had he any confreres?

2ND TORTURER:
    He has been for to preach   full many long years;
    To the people he doth teach   a new law.

1ST TORTURER:
                Sirs, hear's!
    As far as his wit reach,   to new truth he rears.
        When we took him
    We found him in a yard;
    But when I drew out my sword   70
    His disciples grew afeard
        And soon they forsook him.

2ND TORTURER:
    Sir, I heard him say he knew   how to destroy our temple so gay,
    And after build a new   on the third day.

CAIAPHAS:

> How might that be true?　　It took more it to array!
> The masons, I knew　　that hewed it, I say,
> > So wise,
>
> That hewed every stone.

1ST TORTURER:

> Ah, good sir, let him alone!
> He lies like a whetstone:　　　　　　　　　　　　　　　80
> > I give him the prize!

2ND TORTURER:

> The lame runs, the blind sees　　through his false wiles;
> Thus he gets many fees　　from those he beguiles.

1ST TORTURER:

> And men from death he frees　　— they seek him for miles —
> And ever through sorceries　　our sabbath day defiles
> > Evermore, sir.

2ND TORTURER:

> This is his use and custom:
> To heal the deaf and the dumb,
> Wheresoever he doth come;
> > I tell you before, sir.　　　　　　　　　　　　　　　90

1ST TORTURER:

> Men call him a king　　and God's son from on high;
> He would fain down bring　　our laws — if had he his way.

2ND TORTURER:

> Yet is there another thing　　I myself heard him say:
> He sets not a fly's wing　　for Sir Caesar, King for aye —
> > He says thus.
>
> Sir, this same is he
> That excused, with his subtlety,
> A woman taken in adultery —
> > Full well may ye trust us.

1ST TORTURER:

> Sir, Lazarus did he raise　　— that men may perceive —　　100
> When he had lain four days　　dead in his grave.
> All men him praise,　　both master and knave,
> Such witchcraft he makes.

2ND TORTURER:

If he wander and rave

    Any longer
His works may we ban;
For he has changed many a man
Since the time he began,
    And brought us great danger.

1ST TORTURER:

He will not leave it,   though he be culpable.
Men call him a prophet,   a Lord full forcible.   110
Sir Caiaphas, by my wit,   he should be condemnable,
If ye two would, as ye sit,   make it firm and stable
    Together.
For ye two, as I trow,
May defend our law;
That made us to you draw
    And bring this lazy lout hither.

2ND TORTURER:

Sir, I can tell you before,   as I might be harried,
If he reign any more,   our laws are miscarried.

1ST TORTURER:

Sir, if questioned he were,   he would soon be miscarried: 120
That is well seen there   where he has long tarried
    And walked.
He is all sour-looking —
There is somewhat forgotten:
I shall hit on what's rotten,
    By the time we have talked.

CAIAPHAS:

Now fair luck on you fall   for your talking!
For certes, I myself shall   make examining.
(*To* JESUS)
Hearest, harlot, of all?   Of misery may thou sing!
How durst thou thee call   either emperor or king?   130
    I defy thee!
What the devil doest thou here?
Thy deeds will cost thee dear.

Come near and speak in mine ear,
> Or I shall denounce thee.

JESUS *remains silent:* CAIAPHAS *is increasingly enraged.*

Ill luck that thou wast born!   Hark? . . . Says he aught again? . . .
Once before tomorrow morn   to speak you'll be full fain.
This is a great scorn   and no way to explain.
As outlaw hear the horn   till like wolf you are tane,
> Vile, Imposter!   140
To speak one word might make it
Far easier to take it.
Et omnis qui tacet
> *Hic consentire videtur.*

Go on speak one word —   but one, in the devil's name!
Where was thy sire at board   when he met with thy dame?
What, neither booted nor spurred,   and a lord of name?
Speak and shit a turd,   and the devil give thee shame,
> Mr. Come-lightly!
Perdy, if thou were a king,   150
Still might thou be riding.
Fie, on thee, foundling,
> Thou livest only by robbery!

CAIAPHAS *is so puzzled by* JESUS's *silence, that he changes*
tone.

My lad, I am a prelate,   a lord in degree:
I sit in mine state,   as thou may see;
Knights on me wait   in diverse degree.
I might permit thee pride to abate   and kneel on thy knee
> In my presence.
(*He suggests that* JESUS *should offer a bribe*)
As I hope to sing mass
Whoso guards the law, I guess,   160
Will get far more by purchase
> Than he does by just rents.

Further silence brings a return of CAIAPHAS's *anger.*

The devil give thee shame   that ever I knew thee!
Neither blind nor lame —   no one shall pursue thee.

Therefore I shall thee name —   and this will ever rue thee —
"King of Fools" in our game: thus shall I invest thee
       As an imposter.
Darest not speak? Art afeard?
I curse him from whom you learned!
Wei! The devil shit in thy beard,   170
       Vile, false traitor!

Though thy lips be fast stucken,   yet might thou say "mum!".
Bold words has thou spoken: then was thou not dumb.
Be it whole word or broken,   come out with some,
Else on thee vengeance I'll wreaken,   ere news of thy death
                                      come
       All out.
Either hast thou no wit
Or thine ears are unfit.
Why don't you hear it
       When I cry and I shout?   180

ANNAS:

     Ah sir, be not ill paid,   though he not answer.
     He is inwardly flayed —   not "right" up in here.

CAIAPHAS:

     No, but the words he has said   do pain my heart dear.

ANNAS:

     Beware, from justice you've strayed.

CAIAPHAS:

                         Nay! Whiles I live ne'er.

ANNAS:

       Sir, appease you.

CAIAPHAS:

     Foul fortune him befall!

ANNAS:

     Sir, ye are vexed at it all,
     But peradventure he shall
       Hereafter please you.

     We may by our law,   examine him first.   190

CAIAPHAS:

Unless I give him a blow,   my heart will burst!

ANNAS:

Wait till ye his purpose know.

CAIAPHAS:

Nay, but I shall out-thrust

Both his eyes, in a row!

ANNAS:

Sir, ye will not, I trust,

Be so vengeable.

But let me investigate him.

CAIAPHAS:

I pray you — and slay him.

ANNAS:

Sir, we may not destroy him,

Without being condemnable.

CAIAPHAS:

He deserves to be dead: a king he him called.

Ware! Let me gird off his head!

ANNAS:

I hope not ye would.   200

But, sir, do by my reed,   your honour to hold.

CAIAPHAS:

I shall never eat bread,   till that he be stalled

In the stocks!

ANNAS:

Sir, speak soft and still;

Let us do as the law will.

CAIAPHAS:

Nay, I myself shall him kill,

And murder with knocks.

ANNAS:

Sir, think ye that ye are   a man of holy kirk:

Ye should be our teacher,   meekness to work.

CAIAPHAS:
>Yea, but all is out of jar;   and that shall him irk!   210

ANNAS:
>All soft may men go far: in our law is no mirk,
>>I ween.
>Your words are boisterous
>"*Et hoc nos volumus,*
>*Quod de iure possumus*".
>>Ye wot what I mean?

>It is best that we treat him   with fairness.

CAIAPHAS:
>>We? Nay!

ANNAS:
>And so might we get him   some word for to say.

CAIAPHAS:
>Ware! Let me beat him!

ANNAS:
>>Sir, do away!
>For if we thus threat him,   he speaks not this day.   220
>>I beseech:
>If you cease and abide,
>I shall take him aside
>And appeal to his pride
>>To say what he does teach.

CAIAPHAS:
>He has reigned overlong   with his false lies,
>And done mickle wrong: Sir Caesar he defies.
>Therefore shall I him hang,   before I uprise.

ANNAS:
>Sir, the Law wills not he gang   in no kind of wise
>>Unjudged.   230
>But first would I hear
>What he would answer;
>Unless he made any fear
>>Why should be condemned?

>And therefore, an examining   first will I make,
>Since that he calls him a king.

CAIAPHAS:

                              If he that not forsake
    I shall give him a wring,   that his neck shall crack!

ANNAS:

    Sir, ye may not him ding.   No word yet he spake
            That I wist.
    (*To* JESUS)
    Hark, fellow, come near.   240
    Will thou never take care?
    I do marvel thou dare
            Thus do all thine own list.

    But I shall do as the law will,   though the people praise thee.
    Say, did thou aught of this ill?   Can thou aught excuse thee?
    Why standest thou so still   when men thus accuse thee?
    For to hang on a hill,   hark how they boast thee
            To damn!
    Say, art thou God's son from heaven,
    As thou art won't for to namen?   250

JESUS:

    So thyself says, even,
            And right so I am;

    For after this shall thou see   when I do come down
    In brightness on high,   with clouds all around.

CAIAPHAS:

    Ah, ill might the feet be   that brought thee to town!
    Thou art worthy to die.   Say, thief, where is thy crown?

ANNAS:

            Abide, sir.
    Let us lawfully redress.

CAIAPHAS:

    We need no witness;
    Himself says so, express.   260
            Why should I not chide, sir?

ANNAS:

    Was there never man so wick'd   but he might amend
    When it come to the prick,   right as yourself kenned.

CAIAPHAS:

 Nay, sir, but I shall him stick even with mine own hand;
 For if he reign with the quick, we are at an end
   All the same.
 Therefore, whiles I have this breath,
 Let me put him to death.

ANNAS:

 Sed nobis non licet
   Interficere quemquam.   270

 Sir, ye wot better than I we should kill no man.

CAIAPHAS:

 His deeds I defy! His works may we ban;
 Therefore shall he die.

ANNAS:

       Nay, in other ways then,
 And do it lawfully.

CAIAPHAS:

     As how?

ANNAS:

      Tell you I can.

CAIAPHAS:

   Let see!

ANNAS:

 Sir, attend to my saws:
 Men of temporal laws,
 They may doom such a cause;
   And so may not we.

CAIAPHAS:

 My heart is full cold, such a blow was there dealt!   280
 For tales that are told, I burst out of my belt —
 Hardly may it hold my body, if ye it felt!
 Yet would I give of my gold yon traitor to pelt
   Forever.

ANNAS:

 Good sir, do as ye pledged me.

CAIAPHAS:

>Why shall he overset me?
>Sir Annas, if ye stop me,
>>Ye do not your *devoir*.

ANNAS:

>Sir, ye are a prelate.

CAIAPHAS:

>>So may I well seem,
>Myself if I say it.

ANNAS:

>>Be not so extreme.   290
>Men of clerical estate   should no men doom,
>But send them to Pilate.   The temporal law to deem
>>Has he;
>He may best threaten him
>And strongly berate him.
>It will shame you to beat him;
>>Therefore, sir, let be.

CAIAPHAS:

>Fie on him! Be ware!   I am out of my gate.
>Say, why stands he off far?

ANNAS:

>>Sir, he came here of late.

CAIAPHAS:

>No, but I have knights that dare   rap him on the pate.   300

ANNAS:

>Your job is but to scare.   Good sir, abate
>>And hear!
>What need you to chide?
>What need you to flite?
>If ye do yon man smite,
>>Ye are irregular.

CAIAPHAS:

>He that first made me clerk,   and taught me my lore
>From the books that I mark,   the devil give him care!

ANNAS:

    Ah, good sir, hark!   Such words might ye spare.

CAIAPHAS:

    Else would I make short work   of yon rogue and nightmare,   310
        Perdy!
    Before away he is led,
    It would do me some good
    To see knights knock his head
        With knocks two or three.

    For, since he has trespassed   and broken our law,
    Let us make him aghast,   and set him in awe.

ANNAS:

    Sir, as ye'd have in haste,   so shall it be, I trow.
    (*To the* TORTURERS)
    Come and make ready fast,   ye knights in a row,
        Your armament;   320
    And that king to you take,
    And with knocks make him weak.

CAIAPHAS:

    Yea, sirs, and for my sake
        Give him good payment.

    For, if I might go with you —   as I wish that I might —
    I should make mine avow   that once ere midnight
    I should make his head sough   where that I hit right.

1ST TORTURER:

    Sir, dread you not now   of this curséd wight
        Today,
    For we shall so rock him   330
    And with buffets knock him.

CAIAPHAS:

    And look that tightly ye lock him,
        That he run not away.

    For we had better not meet,   if that fellow escape.

2ND TORTURER:

    Sir, let our fault be it,   if we clout not his cap.

CAIAPHAS:
> If ye do as ye say it,   it were a fair hap.

1ST TORTURER:
> Sir, sit ye and see it: we will leave no gap
>> In the feast!
> But, ere we start on this thing,
> Bless us, Lord, with thy ring.   340

CAIAPHAS:
> Now: he shall have my blessing
>> That knocks him the best.

2ND TORTURER:
> Let us work to our note   with this fond fool.

1ST TORTURER:
> We shall teach him, I wot,   a new game of Yool.
> And make him full hot.   Froward, a stool

Enter FROWARD.

> Go fetch us!

FROWARD:
>> Wei, dolt!   Otherways were more dole.
>> And will pinch.
> For the woe that he shall see,
> Let him kneel on his knee.

2ND TORTURER:
> And so shall he, for me.   350
>> Go fetch a small bench.   FROWARD *brings a stool.*

FROWARD:
> Why must he sit soft —   with mickle mischance! —
> That has teened us oft?

1ST TORTURER:
>> Sir, we do all askance.
> If he stand up aloft,   we must hop and dance
> Like cocks in a croft.

FROWARD:
>> Now, a vengeance
>> Come on him!
> As good reason ye show
> As fell with the dew.

Have this: — bear it, you! *He gives the stool to* JESUS.
    Now soon shall we con him.   360

2ND TORTURER:
    Come sir, and sit down.   Must ye be prayed?
    Like a lord of renown,   your seat is arrayed.

1ST TORTURER:
    We shall prove on his crown   the words he has said.

2ND TORTURER:
    There is none in this town,   I trow, be ill paid
           By his sorrow,
    But the father that him got.

1ST TORTURER:
    Now, for aught that I wot
    All his kin cometh too late
           His body to borrow.

2ND TORTURER:
    I wish we were onward.

1ST TORTURER:
                        But his eyes must be hid.   370

2ND TORTURER:
    Yea, if they be not covered,   we lost what we did.
    Step forth then, Froward!

FROWARD:
                    What is now betid?

1ST TORTURER:
    Thou art ever thus wayward.

FROWARD:
                  Have ye none to bid
        But me?
    I may sing "ill-hail"

2ND TORTURER:
    Thou must get us a veil.

FROWARD:
    Ye are ever in one tale.

1ST TORTURER:
>   Now ill luck come to thee!

>   Well had thou thy name,   for thou was ever curst.

FROWARD:
>   Sir, I might say the same   to you, if I durst.   380
>   I have yet my pay to claim: no penny have I pursed.
>   I have had mickle shame,   hunger and thirst,
>   In your service.

1ST TORTURER:
>   Not one word so bold!

FROWARD:
>   Why, it is true that I told
>   And prove it I would.

2ND TORTURER:
>   Thou shall be called to disprove it.

> FROWARD *fetches a blindfold.*

FROWARD:
>   Here, a veil have I found;   I trow it will last.

1ST TORTURER:
>   Bring it hither, good son.   That is it that I asked.

FROWARD:
>   How should it be bound?

2ND TORTURER:
>   About his head cast.   390

1ST TORTURER:
>   Yea, and when it is well wound,   knit a knot fast
>   I reed.   FROWARD *blindfolds* JESUS.

FROWARD:
>   Is it well?

2ND TORTURER:
>   Yea, knave.

FROWARD:
>   What, ween ye that I rave?
>   Christ's curse may he have
>   That last bound his head!

1ST TORTURER:

> Now, since he is blindfold,   I start to begin.
> And thus was I counselled   the mastery to win!

> *He strikes* JESUS.

2ND TORTURER:

> Nay, wrong was thou told.   Thus should thou come in! *Strikes.*

FROWARD:

> I stood and beheld: thou touched not the skin   400
>   But little.

1ST TORTURER:

> How will thou I should do?

2ND TORTURER:

> In this manner: lo!   *Strikes.*

FROWARD:

> Yea, that was well gone to;
>   There starts up a weal. *They strike in turn, repeatedly.*

1ST TORTURER:

> Thus shall we him relieve   of all his fond tales.

2ND TORTURER:

> There's no punch in thy neaf   or else thy heart fails.

FROWARD:

> I can my hand up heave   and knock out the scales.

1ST TORTURER:

> God forbid ye should leave,   but dig in with your nails
>   In a row. *They mock* JESUS *as they scourge him.* 410
> Sit up and prophesy –

FROWARD:

> But make us no lie!

2ND TORTURER:

> Who smote thee last?

1ST TORTURER:

>   Was it I?

FROWARD:

>   He wot not, I trow.

1ST TORTURER:
>   Fast to Sir Caiaphas   go we together.

2ND TORTURER:
>   Rise up, and ill grace!   So, come thou hither.

>   *They drag* JESUS *to* CAIAPHAS.

FROWARD:
>   It seems, by his pace,   he grouches to go thither.

1ST TORTURER:
>   We have given him a graze,   ye may consider,
>   To keep.

2ND TORTURER (*To* CAIAPHAS):
>   Sir, for his great boast   420
>   With knocks he is endorsed!

FROWARD:
>   In faith, sir, we had almost
>   Knocked him to sleep.

CAIAPHAS:
>   Now, since he is well beat,   haste on your gate
>   And tell ye the forfeit   unto Sir Pilate,
>   For he is a judge set   among men of estate;
>   And look ye soon meet.

1ST TORTURER:
>   Come forth, old trot,
>   Be alive!
>   We shall lead thee a trot.

2ND TORTURER:
>   Lift thy feet, can thou not?   430

FROWARD:
>   Then needs me do nought
>   But come after and drive.

>   *Exeunt all except* CAIAPHAS *and* ANNAS.

CAIAPHAS:
>   Alas, now take I heed!

ANNAS:
>   Why mourn ye so?

CAIAPHAS:

> For I am ever in dread,   wondering and woe,
> Lest Pilate, for reward,   let Jesus go.
> But had I slain him indeed,   with these hands two,
>> At once,
> All had been quit then.
> But bribes mar many men:
> Unless he doom truly, then,   440
>> May the devil have his bones!

> Sir Annas, I give you this blame;   for, had ye not been,
> I had made him full tame —   yea, sticked him, I ween,
> To his heart of ill fame   with this dagger so keen.

ANNAS:

> Sir, you must shame   such words for to mean
>> Among men.

CAIAPHAS:

> I will not dwell in this stead,
> But spy how they him lead,
> And pursue him, till dead.
> (*To the audience*)
>> Farewell; we go, men.   *Exeunt.*

Glossary and Notes

appeach: accuse
Armenie: Armenia
askance: jokingly
at one: right now
attaint: convicted
attent: attention
avails: benefits

bale: torment
balk: unploughed
  land
ban: curse
bater: healer
beastis: beasts
Beau sire: fair sir
beforn: before
beginner of blunder:
  i.e., Eve
behest: promised
behests: promises
bell, bear the: are the
  best of all
Benedicité: bless me!
bent: heath
beshrew: curse
betid: happened
bob: cluster, bunch
bone: i.e., carcass
boon: prayer
bragance: bragging
brand: sword
breves: short notes

care: sorrow
carp: prate
carping: prating
cast: trick
cawl: pottage
certes: for sure
chase: hunting
cheek-bone: (trad-
  itionally Abel was
  killed with the jaw-
  bone of an ass)
cheer: face
clean: pure

clergy: learning
clout: cloth (sb.);
  mend (vb.)
crake: make a loud
  noise
croft: yard
crooks: tricks
crown: head/crown
cubit: (an old measure;
  from the elbow to
  tip of the middle
  finger)

dall: fist
dang: struck
daw: fool
devoir: duty
dight: clad, prepared/
  put
dillydon: little darling
ding: are forced
dissever: depart
distance, without:
  undoubtedly
do away: have done
dold: slow, dull
dole: pain, misery/
  charitable gift
Dominus: lord
dote: dotard (sb.);
  talk nonsense (vb.)
dotty-polls: stupid
  heads
dowse: slut

Ecce virgo concipiet:
  behold a virgin
  shall conceive
Ely: Elijah
endorsed: i.e., stamped,
  beaten
engine: contrivance
et hoc . . . possumus:
  and we wish to do
  this because legally
  we are able to

et omnis . . . videtur:
  and all who keep
  silent seem to give
  consent here
even: evening (sb.);
  just(ly), exact(ly),
  calm(ly) (adj., adv.)
eyen: eyes

fain: glad
far cast: clever trick
fare: go
fee: possessions, live-
  stock
fell: moor
firth: forest
flat: level place
fling: run, dash
flit: left, moved
flite: quarrel
fold: sheepfold
forbot: forbid
fordo: destroy
forfeit: offence (sb.);
  offended (vb.)
forfend: forbid
forgang: forego
forlorn: destroyed
forshapen: trans-
  formed
forsooth: truly
forthink: displease
foyn: thrust, blow
free: noble, fine
froward: perverse,
  misshapen
fry: children

gad: go round about,
  wander
gainsay: forbid
gang: go, walk
gar: cause
garcio: varlet
gate: way
gaud: prank

gear: equipment, clothing/business
gin: trap
gird: strike
Gloria in excelsis: Glory to God in the highest
Goodbower: a close, entry from a street, in Wakefield
gossip: godparent
got: begot
griefs: injuries
groat: very small coin (valued 4d.)
grouches: is unwilling
guise: device

hack: trill, sing with many short notes
harbour: home
harlot: rascal
harrow!: help!
hat: called
hent: take hold, catch
hie: hasten
hied: sped
hight: promised
hind: servant
hite: go on
hoar, by my: by my hair
hob-over-the-wall: hobgoblin
Horbury: near Wakefield

ill-hail: bad luck
In nomine . . . Sancti: in the name of God, the Father, Son and Holy Ghost
Isay: Isaiah
iwis: indeed

jangles: chatters
jangling: chattering
Jeremy: Jeremiah
Judas carnas dominus: (a corruption of *laudes canas domino*: sing praises to the lord)

keep: guard
ken: knowledge (sb.); know (vb.)

kenned: knew
kind: offspring, race (sb.); conceived (vb.)
kirk: church
knacked: trilled
knave: boy-servant, boy

land-beggars: vagabonds
lang: long (to do so)
langett: thong
lay: wager
lea: meadow
leach: physician
let: hindrance
lewd: unlearned, stupid
lief: dear, preferred
liefer: rather
list: wish
lord-fast: bound to a lord
lore: lesson
lorn: lose; lost
lozell: rascal
lust: desire

Mahown': Mohammed
mail: bag
manus tuas commendo: into your hands I commend (my spirit)
marked: aimed
marks: coins (valued 13s. 4d.)
meat: food
mede: reward
meiney: company, followers
mess: dish
mickle: much
midden: dung heap
min: less
mind on: remember
mirk: obscurity
mischance: ill luck
mischiefs: misfortunes
morrow: daybreak
mould: earth
muck: dung
munch-pins: teeth

nails, our dear God's: i.e., the nails of Christ's cross
namen: name (sb.); speak, say (vb.)

neaf: fist
near-hands: nearly
nesh: soft
Nichol Neddy: Nick the Needy (derisive)
nonce: once
note: work/fuss

otherwhile: at other times
out-thring: burst out
owe: ought

page: boy, lad
panier: large basket
paramour: passionately
Paternoster: Lord's prayer
peeps: cries
perdy: by God, for sure
Pickharness: literally, one who robs men killed in battle; a thief
po: peacock
poll: shear
Pontio Pilato: Pontius Pilate
pottle: two quarts
powdered: seasoned
prick: point
purchase: illegal means
purveyance: requisition

quick, the: the living

race: torrent, rush
reck: care
recure: recover
reed: counsel (sb.); advise, think (vb.)
reel: move at speed
reproof: disgrace
re-stored: filled again
resurrex a mortuus: i.e. *resurrexit a mortuis* (He rose from the dead; from the Creed)
rood: cross
runagates: vagabonds, rascals

sans: without
Sarceny: land of the Saracens

saw: saying, words
sayn: say
scale: drinking-cup
scapethrift: spendthrift
*sed nobis . . . quem-
    quam*: but it is not
    lawful for us to put
    any man to death
    (*John*, 18.31)
semblance: looks
shame: disgrace
shank: leg
shoon: shoes
shower: sharp pain
shrew: villain (sb.);
    curse (vb.)
Sibyl: the Erythraean
    Sibyl (who was said
    to have prophesied
    Christ's birth)
skant: scarcity
skelp: slap
slake: assuage, relieve
sleight: trick
sooth: truth (sb.);
    true (adj., adv.)
soothly: truly
sough: throb
sounds: straits
space: time
spell: speech (sb.);
    give news (vb.)
spitous: spiteful
spot: blemish
springs: travels
spurn: stub
Stafford blue: a blue
    cloth (i.e., Noah
    should be beaten
    black and blue)
stall: place, station/
    throne
stark: stiff
starne: star
stead: place (sb.);
    pressed (vb.)
steer-tree: helm

steyven: voice
sticked: stabbed
still: silence (sb.);
    continually/quietly
    (adv.)
stint: shut up
store: livestock
store, in: in reserve
stot: heifer
stout: valiant
stucken: shut
sudden: unexpected
swelt: pass out, am
    about to die
swink: toil

tane: taken
teen: sorrow, affliction
    (sb.); trouble (vb.)
temporal: secular
tend: pay, offer
tenory: tenor
tent: notice, attention
theretil: about it
thrall: slave
thraw, a: for a while
throng: pressed together
thwang, many a: a
    flogging
tide: time
tidely: quickly
tod, on my: alone
token: omen
tooth: i.e., accent
tree: piece of timber
trot: hag
trow: think, believe
*trust from thee may
    borrow*: may take
    it from you as true
tup: male sheep
tyr: (shepherd's call to
    sheep)

uncouthly: strangely
uneven: at odds, at
    sixes and sevens

*Virgo concipiet . . .
    pariet*: a virgin shall
    conceive and bear a
    son

wain: waggon
waltering: sprawling
warlock: powerful
    adversary (i.e. Satan)
wat: know
wedder: wether, ram
weed: clothing
ween: think
Wei!: (an exclamation
    of surprise, sorrow
    or emphasis)
wend: go
Wey-allay!: Alas!
whop: (shepherd's call
    to turn sheep)
whyr: (shepherd's call
    to sheep)
widder: wither
wight: creature, person
wise: way, manner
wist: knew
wit: understanding (sb.),
    know (vb.)
wode: mad
wot: know
wreak: injury (sb.);
    avenge (vb.)
wryers: quarrellers

yare: ready
yelp: boasting
Yool, game of: hot
    cockles (a game of
    blindfold)
Yorktown: ("Kemp-
    town" in the manu-
    script; John Kemp
    was Archbishop of
    York, 1426-53)

Zachary: Zacharias